THE SHADOW MAN

THE SHADOW MAN

I SAW WHAT LAW ENFORCEMENT DIDN'T SEE

ALAN VINNICOMBE

THE CHRIS WATTS CASE

Wisconsin Whispers

The Shadow Man
I Saw What Law Enforcement Didn't See
The story they don't want you to know
Copyright © 2021 by Alan Vinnicombe

www.wisconsinwhispers.com
www.wisconsinwhispersUK.com

Join AD on YouTube
https://www.youtube.com/c/ArmchairDetectiveBLUE

Unless otherwise notated, all quotes from the personal dialogue are
from the public discovery from Weld County, Colorado, DA's office.

ISBN: 9780578986913
Cover design by JCMf
Book Cover art and logo copyright © 2021 by Alan Vinnicombe

First Printing, 2021

Dedication

I am grateful to dedicate this book to my family and friends that have supported me throughout this journey. I've spent hours watching, talking, and comparing specific details of this case. My moderators and subscribers are what helped keep the investigation alive. Together, we found things that didn't add up. Once you see something, you can't unsee it.

I dedicate this book to those who have not ever given up on believing that other individuals were involved other than Chris Watts. Law enforcement provided us with enough information that proves others should have been questioned and investigated more than they were initially.

Most of all, I dedicate this book to my loving family.

Forever in our Hearts
We love You
Miss Trudy Richards

Justice for Shanann, Bella, Celeste, and Nico

Contents

Foreword

The story they don't want you to read. One man's journey to find the metadata in the infamous case of Christopher Lee Watts.

On August 13, 2018, life changed for many people. A family had their lives stolen.

The man that was sentenced for this crime was shockingly their husband and father, Christopher Watts.

This news made international headlines. It was the case that held a place in many hearts.

A British man in the U.K. named Alan Vinnicombe was studying cases. Alan had a genuine concern for the victims of murder. One of the cases was the notorious missing person case of Madeleine McCann. The young British girl went on holiday to Portugal with her parents and didn't come home. Alan spent over a decade diligently studying this case. Looking for answers and looking for Madeleine.

Alan has a unique talent for studying the metadata, and he used this on Facebook and social media for this case.

Alan has spent his life as a talented businessman, a father, and a grandfather. He has had many businesses and traveled the world playing in major poker tournaments. The latter has helped him be able to read people and their "tells." Being a poker player is much more than luck. You must be able to study people and watch them, taking in the smallest details.

Alan noticed the Christopher Watts case in 2018 and decided to make a YouTube channel to help many cases and bring awareness to the victims of crime.

Being diligent and a man who likes to study, he sat and watched hours of the footage released by Weld County. Hour after hour.

Meanwhile, a movement was building up online to blame Shannan Watts for murdering her own children. This tore at Alan's heartstrings, and he wasn't having it.

He took it upon himself to find a way to vindicate Shannan.

One day on January 10th, 2019, which also by some fate happened to be Shannan's birthday, he released a premiere on his YouTube channel. Alan had spotted a small shadow under the truck in the driveway that morning. He was the first person to release this on YouTube.

This book is the story of that shadow and the story of Alan's incredible journey of how he built his YouTube channel from nothing. He took on American Law enforcement who don't take kindly to being proven wrong.

This book is for those that have not heard of or followed the Watts case. Alan uses the first few chapters to narrate the exact events during and the day after the murders.

He will then be adding to the events his discoveries and, more importantly, things that are, without a doubt, questionable.

"We have stepped on some big toes. From now on, we have to tiptoe to Justice."

Chapter 1

Murder Monday

In the early hours of August 13, 2018, a young father backs his work truck up into his driveway, inching into the door of his three-car garage in suburban Colorado. He stops, and most of the truck is visible on his next-door neighbor's security camera. He is wearing a long-sleeved, black shirt with sleeves pushed up over his forearms and loosely fitting jeans. He walks back and forth from his truck to the garage several times and loads items into the cab as well as the bed of his truck. Darkness fades as the sun brightens the sky into the day.

He loaded a red gasoline can into the bed of his truck. He then removes it and turns to walk back into the garage, only to turn around again. He decides to walk all the way around the front of the truck to the driver's side. Then he places the gas can in the bed of the 2015 Ford Super Duty F250 in Caribou Metallic, which runs on compressed natural gas. Unlike most days, where he walks out to his truck parked on the street with his lunch and backpack, it takes him a very long time to get on the road that morning. It seems strange to his next-door neighbor, who is friendly with him and his family. He could not recall a single morning before this day when he pulled his truck into the driveway.

The man works in the oil industry, and his wife prefers him to park on the street, not to stain the driveway with oil. Also, the garage door is loud, and the girls are light sleepers. He goes straight into the field that morning to investigate an incident at one of the sites under his supervision, so he does not go into the office first as he normally would. He leaves at 5:46 am. He calls several coworkers beginning at 6:29 am, asking which site they will be heading out to first.

After three unanswered calls to a co-worker named Kodi, he sends a text message. The site is in a rural area where cellular reception is not reliable.

He sends a text to Kodi at 6:31 am, "Where you at?"

Just a minute later, Kodi replied, "Just got fuel in Kersey."

He tries by phone again with no answer. He sends two more text messages to Kodi at 6:33 am, letting him know he is in Cervi and asking which site he will first. Kodi Roberts replies," DPC state."

Two minutes later, Kodi sends another text: "I need to call Chad and see if he plans on still stroking the 10-29 out there to see if it will pump up. If so, I'll have to meet him, or he will have to get the cannon plugs from Tony, OK?"

"Ok. Let me know before I leave here."

"I think he might be heading out there today.

The phone was breaking up pretty bad."Kodi added.

At 6:39 am, he tried to get a hold of Chad by phone, but there was no answer. Then, he texts him, "You headed out to Cervi? I'm out here; Kodi said something about pumping up the 10-29."

"Well, since you're out there, you want to fire it up? Have Kodi bring his cables." Chad answered.

"Ok, I will." He agreed.

"I'll head that way in a bit." Chad texted.

The GPS Geotab service on his work truck shows he pulled in, stopped, and parked at Cervi 319 at 6:53 am.

At 6:59 am, Kodi informed him that he would head out to the 10-29 and then Chad would meet them there.

Cervi ranch was a mix of both the wonder of nature blended with gigantic monuments to 20th-century industrialism. Two large oil tanks are enclosed in fences surrounding a vast open space of terrain spotted with colorful wildflowers.

This hardworking father could certainly take a moment to enjoy a brief gaze out at the ranch and wonder at its natural beauty. He liked being an operator and getting to work out in the fields. He always enjoyed working with his hands, but his real passion was in the automotive industry.

He used to be a mechanic who had dreamed of working in NASCAR as a pit crew member. He even went to technical school at the NASCAR Academy to earn his mechanical certification. The oil industry was not such a bad gig, and the money was good. Plus, carpal tunnel symptoms made it painful and uncomfortable to work on cars all day.

Nearly 20 minutes go by, and the man takes a photo on his personal cell phone of his computer screen while sitting in his truck. At 7:40 am, he sends his wife of 6 years a message that reads, "If you take the kids somewhere, please let me know where they are at!"

Then he makes a two-and-a-half-minute call to Troy, another field supervisor. Just a minute later, Kody texts him and says, "I'm here at the 10-29. Do you mind coming out here just in case something goes sideways?"

"Yea. I am at 3-19. One sec." He then takes a picture at 7:43 am of two black steel pipes sticking up vertically from beneath the ground. The left pipe was surrounded by an area of darkened dirt and gravel that reached the edge of the pipe on the right. He has isolated the pipe that warranted his attention at Cervi3-19 first thing in the morning. It should be an easy fix. He calls his supervisor, Luke Epple, and holds a two-minute conversation.

Kodi asks him a few minutes later, "is it a lot?" He sends the photo of the pipes.

"Want me to bring some Gator? We can try and pressure test the lines too if you want?"

Kodi had been the one to report the issue at 3-19 the previous Friday.

He replies at 7:55, "I got it handled. Thanks, though."

30 minutes go by, and he tries calling his wife again. He searches online for his girls' school so he can call. They attend

a private, nationally accredited Primrose preschool, boasting highly educated board members and industry experts who developed an extensive early childhood learning curriculum. He tells staff that the girls will no longer be attending school there. Then asks if they were dropped off that morning.

Around this time, he is joined at 3-19 Chad and a newer employee named Melissa, who had only worked there for a few months. By this time, he has a shovel in hand and is digging a small hole about 12 inches wide and six to eight inches deep near one of the tanks.

He greets the two, and they have a conversation about the events of the prior weekend. He talks about a Colorado Rockies game he went to on Saturday. He hired a babysitter because his wife was out of town on business. Minutes later, a full-faced man in his thirties with a full dark beard named Troy arrives.

As he repairs the equipment, he releases the pressure on the valve, causing some oil to spit out. Melissa and Chad head out to another site.

Melissa finds it strange that he went directly to the field that morning because it is customary to go to the Anadarko office first and then head out in teams. She also realizes that he did not send a group message to the team that he was at 3-19 as was the common practice in their line of work.

She also notes he is wearing an older pair of work boots with his jeans tucked in. When she asks, he explains he is worried about the snakes and "legless lizards." She would return to that site later in the day to notice the repairs had not been completed. This was out of character because he had a propensity for cleaning up spills. She and Chad would also return the next day to check the equipment.

At 9:05, a reminder alerts for his wife's obstetrician appointment on her phone. She is fifteen weeks pregnant with their third child, a boy, they would call Nico. They already have two young daughters named Bella, aged four, and Celeste, called CeCe, aged three.

At this moment, her husband calls Ann, their Realtor, and they carry a three-minute and forty-second conversation. Usually, it is his wife that contacts her.

His wife is contacted by Centura Health Physicians Group at 10:06 am, and they leave a voicemail message.

At 10:10 am, he searches Google for the song "Battery" by his favorite band Metallica.

Pounding out aggression
Turns into obsession
Can not kill the battery
Cannot kill the family
Battery is found in me

At 10:28 am, he receives a message from his mother-in-law asking if his wife is okay. They hold a one-minute conversation following this message.

He spends eight minutes searching the internet for hotels in Aspen, Colorado. He and his wife were planning a romantic weekend getaway to reconnect. The two had been having some marital issues and his wife, Shanann, thought it would be beneficial to get away from the daily grind of working-parent life to spend some quality time together without the girls.

He places a nearly two-minute phone call to the Westin Snowmass Resort. After the call, he receives another brief phone call from his mother-in-law.

He searches the web for the contact information for Groupon, a company that partners with businesses offering deals to help build their clientele.

He calls her mom back again at 10:51 am.

Shortly after, the group at Cervi 3-19 leaves and heads over to Union Pacific Railroad Company 10-29, as they had discussed. At some point thereafter, as Troy would later recall, the young father started receiving Ring doorbell notifications that his wife's friend, Nickole, had been there at his house.

He speaks with Nickole a few times, during which she expresses immense concern that Shanann has not answered any of her calls or texts. This is very alarming because Nickole is Shanann's very close friend and a rep who works under her at Le-Vel, direct sales health and wellness company whose flagship product line is Thrive. The Thrive system consists of vitamin capsules, dermal fusion patches, shakes, and bars.

Shanann is always on her phone networking or uploading videos to Facebook. Nickole was also expecting to hear how the doctor's appointment went that morning, so it was very disconcerting that Shanann had suddenly gone completely silent.

The man tries to reassure Nickole that Shanann plans to go on a playdate with the girls and not worry.

The man is Christopher Lee Watts, currently serving five life sentences for the murders of his wife and two daughters in Wisconsin's Dodge Correctional Facility.

Chapter 2

The Phone Goes Silent

Nickole had spent the weekend with Shanann and some other employees of Le-Vel in Arizona. Shanann was not quite like herself. She is usually bright and energetic. This weekend, she was broken. She spoke of issues in her marriage with her friends on this trip, and as her team leader Addy recalled, Shanann was a wreck.

Her husband seemed less than thrilled over the pregnancy with their third child, Nico. There was a $62.00 credit card charge on August 11 that caused alarm. Shanann was suspicious and checked the menu for pricing, determining that the total should have been half for a salmon dinner and a beer.

Addy tried to reassure Shanann that maybe he had bought some beer for his friends and that Chris would never cheat on her. Chris had plans to go to the Rockies game and must have stopped into the Lazy Dog for something to eat. She texted Chris to save his receipts so they could write them off on their taxes.

Shanann laments that he had been distant, not showing any affection to Shanann over their summer vacation to North Carolina, where the couple was born and raised. He joined his family after 5 weeks and spent the last week of the trip with her family on Myrtle Beach. She had been vomiting and feeling unwell, and Chris would normally be at her beck and call. One evening she was so sick that her brother stayed up all night caring for her. Chris stayed out on the couch.

Shanann had Lupus, a chronic autoimmune disease in which the immune system attacks healthy tissue. Her previous pregnancies had been complicated. Their oldest child Bella was considered a miracle baby. For her pregnancy with CeCe, her parents moved to Colorado and stayed with the family for 15 months. They conceived relatively easily with Nico, but Shanann seemed quite ill, nonetheless.

The girls also had some medical issues, including asthma and allergies. Celeste had an abnormally narrow esophagus at birth which required surgical interventions. As a result, there were considerable medical debts that had negatively impacted their financial stability.

This past weekend the friends in Arizona all noted a marked change in Shanann's demeanor. Shanann was very open with her workmates. Nickole, Addy, and Cassie were all aware of the issue between Shannan and Chris. She was unwell emotionally as well as physically. Addy drove Shanann and Nickole to the airport around 5:45 to 6:00 pm, Arizona time, on Sunday the 12th. Nickole dropped Shanann off at her front door at 1:48 am Monday and drove away.

Later Monday morning, no one has heard from Shanann at all. She had an appointment scheduled for baby Nico, and her friends are wondering how the appointment went. She missed that appointment. Considering the circumstances, Nickole decides to drive over to Shanann's house to check on her. No answer.

Nickole and her son, Nick, notice the Lexus in the garage with the child seats installed. Nickole tries to enter the house, but it is latched from the inside. She calls Chris and asks him to come home to check on his wife. She is concerned about Shanann's blood sugar, thinking maybe she has passed out. She and her son attempt all the doors and windows, unable to enter the home.

Addy asks Chris at 12:31 that afternoon: "Everyone is worried. It's not like her not to respond, and we haven't heard from her all day."

Chris then calls Nickole, and they have a 40-second conversation.

At 12:43, Cassie contacts Chris, "Shanann is in a very bad way emotionally, and I'm worried about her. I know you are having issues, but I don't know {to} what extent, but I do know I have never seen her so broken, and I am worried."

To that, Chris replied," She went to a friend's house with the kids, and she won't tell me where. When I get home, I will update you."

A few minutes later, Cassie explains to Chris: "Sweetie, nobody knows about you and her other than Nicki and me, so where would she go if not with Nicki and not to Arizona where I'm at? Her car and shoes and everything is at the house. What the heck is going on with you guys that she would totally shut out everything? It's not like her."

"I told Nicki about it so she wouldn't freak out anymore at the house. I think Christina knows as well. We talked last night, and I told her I wanted to sell the house, get something smaller. Separation would be best right now if we could work thru the issues. I really don't want you to think I'm a bad person Cassie."

"Right now, I don't care about you, or your relationship, or what type of person you are or not, or what I think of you, and I'm not trying to be rude when I say that." Cassie was losing her patience.

"I'm going home, Cassie. On my way. Don't call the police. I will be there in 45 minutes." Chris assures.

"Nicki and I know what state she was in all weekend, and we want to see if she isn't in the house because this is seriously a concern."

At 2:11 pm, Chris texted Shanann, "Where are you?"

A few minutes later, text messages from Nickole to Shanann's phone begin to flood in.

"Just wanted to see if you were ok. I know you were hurting last night. Hope you're ok".

"Let me know how your appointment goes."

"I have been to your house, and you won't open your door, your alarm is set, your shoes are sitting inside, your car's home, I am so very concerned about you right now. Please text me or call me and tell me you're OK. If you don't want to talk to nobody, you don't want to be around nobody, I get it, it's fine, but I need to know you're OK."

Chapter 3

August 13, 2018
1340 Hours

Officer Scott Coonrod of the Frederick Police department is dispatched to 2825 Saratoga Trail for a well-being check of Shanann Watts, a pregnant female born 01-10-1984. Nickole called about her friend who is

15 weeks along and not feeling well. She was not answering calls and had missed a doctor's appointment.

Coonrod meets Nickole and her two children in front of Shannon's house, trying to gain entry. Nickole, a round woman with burgundy hair, is dressed in an olive green graphic printed shirt and wearing white-rimmed sunglasses on top of her head.

Nickole keys in the code to unlock the door, but the latch on the home's interior prevented it from opening more than three inches. Coonrod announces himself but hears no noises coming from inside.

The group peers into windows, looking for signs of Shanann and the girls. Nickole continues to call Chris, asking him to come home. Each time, a different arrival time for Chris is reported. Coonrod calls Chris and asks for the code to open the garage door. Chris said the code did not work and he would be there in 5 minutes.

Chris arrives in his third outfit for the day, going out of his way to stop briefly at 6507 Black Mesa Drive, a vacant, newly built home about four blocks west of his house. He now has on a gray shirt, still with the long sleeves pushed up.

He enters the home through the garage, stopping and opening the passenger side door briefly before going into the house. He squats down for a moment, then rises and shuts the door to go inside the house. To onlookers, it appears as though he may be picking something up from the car before he goes inside.

One minute and five seconds later, he opens the front door to allow Officer Coonrod, Nickole, and her two children into the house. Nickole slowly walks to the kitchen on her phone, and the officer looks through doors and around corners seeing if he can locate Shanann. The family dog Dieter, a Dachshund, barks at Coonrod.

"You checked upstairs? I just wanted to make sure she wasn't passed out. Is she diabetic? Do you mind if I look around?" asks Coonrod.

"Go ahead." Dieter continues to bark at Coonrod.

Chris tells the dog to go outside.

"Oh, you're fine." Coonrod says to Dieter.

Coonrod is wearing an Axon Body Cam documenting his movements through the house, opening and closing doors to the sprawling, 5-bedroom home. He goes to the basement, sees workout equipment, storage containers, a trampoline, and an unmade bed. The basement is rather well lit due to its many windows, letting the sunlight pour in from above. Coonrod ascends the stairs to the house's first level, then continues up to the second floor. Coonrod speaks into his radio, "Checking the house per consent."

"She's not at home," Chris announces.

"Well, shoot." Coonrod retorts. He checks the laundry room, asks Chris if she has any friends she may be hanging out with, and asks about her parents, who he understands live out of state.

"Across the country, North Carolina," Chris replies. "Yeah, so that's not happening."

Chris continues, "All the girl's blankies are gone." "Um."

"Their blankies they sleep with; they don't leave anywhere without them."

"Okay," Coonrod replies, making a mental note.

He goes into each of the girls' brightly colored bedrooms with his flashlight shining in on every corner.

"Nothing else appears to be missing, though, just the stuff you would take for a quick trip?"

Coonrod walks back into the loft area.

"Her phones here? Her phones here!" Nickole exclaims as she climbs the stairs.

"Does she work?" Coonrod asks Chris. "Yeah. She works from home."

"Oh, from home?"

"She works- this is her lifeline," Chris says, holding up Shanann's phone.

"That thing is probably about to start blowing up!" Nick comments.

"And it was shut down?" Coonrod asks. "Yeah."

Nickole paces frantically while holding her phone in a con-versation. She walks into the playroom. Nick also paces, avoid-ing eye contact with Chris.

Nick says to his mother, "Well, it was originally on the couch under the pillow."

"Do you know her passcode?" Chris directs his question to a pacing Nickole.

"Um, I don't know her passcode." Nicky answers.

"It used to be 2385, and now it is 6 digits!" Chris states with a tinge of annoyance.

"It's the baby's due date!" Nicole exclaims.

"1-31-8-19..." Chris trails off as the phone has finally been accessed.

"What did she do for work?" Coonrod continues asking Chris.

"She worked for a direct sales company called Thrive," Chris answered as he finally unlocked his wife's phone.

Nickole heads back to the playroom. The tension in the room is palpable. Chris starts reading through the contents of Shanann's phone while Nickole anxiously clutches her chest.

Several moments pass: "How often does her blood sugar drop low?" asks Coonrod.

"Cassie, her friend that was in Arizona, she said that. And that's the first time it's ever happened...."

Nickole tells how Cassie was a nurse and suspected Shanann had low blood sugar and has a history of migraines, especially during this past weekend in Arizona. She explained how she was not eating as she normally would, only taking a few bites, and said she was full. Nickole nervously checks her phone. A Thrive patch adheres to the back of her left hand.

"She doesn't ever blackout or has a history of seizures or anything like that?" Coonrod inquires.

"No, I mean she...." Chris begins. "I mean a long, long, long, long time ago. She got in a car wreck. I believe that's what happened, but Imitrex is something she takes for migraines." Chris begins.

"She took more Imitrex in the last month than she ever has before. That's just because of North Carolina and the humidity and everything like that. She was there for 6 weeks, and we got back Tues- Monday, or Tuesday. And then she flew out to Arizona Friday, Friday morning," he decides, and then she got back last night. At about 2 am, her flight got delayed... She left about 11:00 and got here at 2:00. I went to work this morning at about 5:15, 5:30." Chris blinks twice before Coonrod carries on.

"What do you do?"

"I work in oil and gas at Anadarko."

"What do you do for them?" Coonrod asks."Operator."

"Oh. Long days then?"

"Yeah, I'd definitely still be out there. It's always a long day, especially in that heat." Chris looks down at his phone.

Nickole continues pacing the room while stroking her hair away from her face in a soothing gesture and continues to make calls.

Chris and Nickole both look at Shanann's phone and realize neither is touching it now.

Nickole is still on her phone, shifting her weight from side to side. Chris walks back up to Shanann's phone resting on the half-wall ledge. Nickole glances suspiciously at the phone.

"And there's calls or text messages?" Chris says to Nickole.

"Can you look at your camera and see in your security system...see when she left?" Nicole asks.

"Unless they left out the front door...."

Nickole interrupts, "Because you told me she went on a playdate with the girls."

"That is what she told me." He interrupts.

"Addy says you told her she left in the middle of the night."

"She went with some friends...she left to go to a friend's house *with the kids*. That's why they weren't in school." Chris explains, sensing Nickole's suspicion.

"Addy says you told her she left in the middle of the night."

Nickole is anxiously trying to make a phone call.

She turns away from Chris. His story is not adding up.

"Oh no. She didn't leave in the middle of the night. No." He laughs.

She walks back to the playroom and answers her phone. "Yeah?"

Coonrod asks Chris, "Where do your kids go to school at?"

"Primrose in Vista Ridge"

Nickole walks up to Chris and hands him her phone. "Sandy wants to talk to you." officer.

"Hey." He answers and turns away from the "Yeah. So, she was at a friend's house...that's what she told me, "His voice trails off as he walks to the back corner of the loft.

"I have no clue...none whatsoever why she wouldn't take her cell phone." He walks into another room. "Yeah, I can take a look at that and see...but it's so random because it goes on and on...they told me it was open when I got here...."

He continues walking back and forth as he carries on this phone conversation. "It doesn't make any sense at all." He explains to his mother-in-law.

"I am at a loss for...I don't know- I don't know where she's at or where the kids are at."

Coonrod remains fixed on Chris as he tries to glean information from the conversation "Only people out of state that she would contact would be in Arizona."

Coonrod takes the opportunity to continue peeking through the rooms upstairs, flashlight in hand. He looks in on a brightly painted lavender bedroom to the right of the banister overlooking the staircase.

Nickole's teenage son Nick comes up the stairs, explaining how the next-door neighbor has security footage. "The guy with the camera said no one left the house during the day! The only people who showed up to the driveway and entered were us." He reports that the only people in the driveway were Chris leaving for work and Nickole when she dropped off Shanann at 1:48 am.

THE SHADOW MAN ~ 21

"I can see if I can get on the USAA app and Chase app. I'll see...I will, I will. Alright, here's Nicki." Chris ends his conversation on the phone.

Coonrod radios dispatch to cancel medical they were staged. Nickole is on the phone, opens her mouth to speak but changes her mind and walks downstairs.

Coonrod can hear the alerts as Chris sends text messages.

"What time do you work?"

"Usually, I... by the time I get to work, it's about 6:30 'til 3:30, 4:00."
"Do you work nights or days?" "Days."

"What time did you leave today?"

"Leave there or here?" Chris points off to the right and then down.

"Here." Replies Coonrod.

"Usually about 5:30 or 6." Chris Watts, when asked about this specific day in time, he begins his reply with the word 'Usually.'

Coonrod seems to glance over this slight variance from his earlier timeline. "Was Shanann here then?"

"Yes."

"Does she usually watch the kids, or do you have a daycare to watch them?"

"She usually watches the kids if they're not at school."

"Okay." Coonrod has finished this line of questioning. More long seconds tick away in absolute silence. Chris taps away frantically on his phone. Nickole mentions something from downstairs about the pool. "At the pool?" Chris repeats.

"That little center thing down there?"

Coonrod is asking about the Wyndham Hill Clubhouse.

"Yeah. There's a pool down there." Chris verifies.

"I have been here like, off and on, 3 hours...and nothing," Nickole interjects.
"I mean- I can look out there and check," Chris suggests.

Coonrod changes the subject. "You guys having any issues, like marital issues, or?"

"We're going through a separation."

"You are? Like have you guys filed yet or anything, or are you just talking?"Coonrod continues.

"No, we were going to sell the house, then we were going to separate." he trails off.

"Now, how is that going? Civil for the most part?"

"Civil." Chris taps his fingers nervously on his phone during the questioning.

"Does your wife go to that swimming pool often?" Coonrod asks, referring to the neighborhood pool.

"That depends. On a hot day like this, I would think no."

Nickole is talking with her younger child downstairs. Chris paces and continues thumbing through his iPhone.Several minutes go by.

"It says 5:27 am the overhead garage door was left open and never shut. So, either I pulled away and shut the door, it never shut. It was shut when you got here?" He looks to Nickole. "The sensor was tripping out, which has happened before-I had had to replace it about two weeks ago before I left. It said the basement door was left open at 5:26. Visitor detected at 1:48. That's when she got home." He lists the alerts out of sequence, blazing past the basement door alert as quickly as possible.

Chris mentions something about an alert at 12:10."That is when you came."

Nickole is gazing at a sunset photo and a family caricature on the wall as she anxiously fidgets with her bottom lip.

"Are you able to pull up the video of the 12:10?

Was it the front door?" Coonrod asks excitedly. "At 12:10... that was Nicki," Chris explains.

"That was me," says Nickolas. She looks up from her phone.

"Oh? That was you? Okay." Coonrod is disappointed that the 12:10 alert reveals no clues to Shanann and the girls' whereabouts.

"And it was beeping at me out in the field," Chris added.

Chris sets his phone down on the black shelf outside the master bedroom. He walks into the bedroom and walks out a moment later with something on the tip of his left index finger. It's Shanann's wedding ring.

Chapter 4

Definitely an Odd One

"Is that her wedding ring Chris?" Nickole gasps.

The two paces and text frantically as Coonrod looks on. "Yeah."Several more minutes go by.

"Does she do her work from a laptop?" Coonrod asks.

"Phone." Chris and Nickole answer simultaneously.

"Just from the phone," Coonrod says.

"What about your banking apps?" Nickole asks astutely.

"I have tried- her logins are different than mine...."

"It's not a joint account?" Asks Coonrod.

Chris continues, "It's not a different account; it's a joint account, but like she controls all of it because she doesn't let me do the finances. I was horrible back in the day, so she just kind of handles all of that. She does it. I have the apps on my phone, but I don't have her login."

"Can't you log into your account, though?" Nickole persists.

"No, I don't have a laptop. Her log in, I don't know her log in. I know the password. It was always the same password...." Chris explains. The three decide the bank account info would be very useful to see if she bought something.

"What days does she typically do work?" Coonrod asks.

"All day, every day." Chris, again, trails off.

"Every day? What was the name of the company again?"

"Le-Vel.L-E-V-E-L."

"Where are they based out of?"

"Memphis. They don't have, like, an office." Chris begins.

"Does she have somebody that she reports to, though?"

"Um, she has her leaders, but they're both in the northeast part of the country.

She has Addy. She has Amanda. She has Sam." Chris defers to Nickole, looking for her to chime in. Chris continues pacing back and forth in front of the officer.

"Do you have her phone number?" Coonrod asks.

"Addy's?"Nickole asks. "Yeah."
Nickole gives him the number.

Chris grabs the ledge next to the stairs and swallows hard. He uses his sleeve to wipe the sweat from his face. Nickole stands a few feet away from him, her chin resting on her hand as she waits for someone to speak next or make a move.

Coonrod ventures across to the master bedroom, where a darkly finished, four-poster bed is centered beneath the elegant drop ceiling. The bed is stripped down to the mattress.

"And there was no note by the wedding ring?" Coonrod inquires.

"No. I put it back where it was." Chris replied.

"Is any of her clothes or anything like that missing?" Coonrod walks around the bed, past a pile of laundry. Their dark curtains hung from each window, blocking out the sunlight on this hot summer afternoon. He steps into the master bathroom. Then, finally joining Chris in the neatly organized, purple-painted closet, he asks, "It didn't look like she picked up a bag?

"It would be kind of hard to tell," Chris explains, waving his hand at the neatly organized, color-grouped array of blouses and hats. "It would be easy to tell if, like, she took a lot. It's hard to tell if it's just a little bit or not."

"Okay. Did she tell you anything about leaving or moving out?" Coonrod tries to understand.

"Not moving out. I mean, the last time I talked to her this morning, she said she was going to take the kids to a friend's house, and that's where she was going to be." Chris narrated, emphasizing certain points in the sequence of his story with hand gestures.

"...And then I text her today and never heard anything." His eyes are fixed on officer Coonrod, searching for approval. He continues, "The car is here- the car is here. The car seems to be here. Unless someone came here and picked her up but the people that I know...."

He raises his eyebrows; "Nobody's heard from her. Nobody's seen her." He states in a mysterious tone.

"Right." Coonrod agrees uncomfortably. He changes the subject. "Who do you guys' bank with?"

Barely blinking, he licks his lips. "Chase and USAA." Chris begins rocking nervously, shifting his body weight from side to side, biting his bottom lip.

Coonrod exits the closet." Definitely an odd one."

"I don't know what I should do right now. Should I drive around like the normal route that she would be?" Chris suggests.

"Where does she normally go to?" Coonrod asks.

"I mean, just like drive where she would normally take the kids to school. Um, people that I know that live down, like Kristen, lives down that way. That's the only people, the only routes I know she would really take."

"Does she go to their house frequently?"

"Not much, but...." His phone rings. "Hey. I'm still talking with the officer right now. Okay bye. I will, definitely. Alright, bye." He disconnects the call. "Sorry about that. That was her mom." Chris explains. "Do you think it's smart just to go like drive around and see if like?" Chris blinks slowly and smiles widely at his second brazen attempt to flee the situation.

"Probably not, cause you don't know what car she's in or where she's at. I mean, obviously, you're not going to see her car. It's here." Coonrod advises. Chris looks down and away, defeated, briefly shaking his head.

"What about Sara?" Nicole exclaims, listing off another of Shanann's Friends. Chris looks off to the left, blinks twice, and looks back down to his phone.

Nickole says to Chris, "Well, I know Amanda is out of town." Chris turns his attention back down to his phone as Nickole speaks. He holds the phone up to his ear, presumably trying to make a call.

"I don't know anything else I can do." He says in a small voice, with pleading eyes open wide as he implores officer Coonrod. "Just wait for her here?" Watts has his phone held up to his ear.

"I've got my detective coming because this is an odd situation," Coonrod advises. Never have truer words been uttered. "You want to try to get her pinpointed down, find a friend or something."

"Okay."

"He may have you call the bank," Coonrod advises.

They begin the walk down the stairs, stopping at the top couple of steps. Chris connects with Sara, a friend of Shanann's, on the phone. "Hey Sara, it's Chris Watts. Not too bad. Have you heard from Shanann today?" He pauses for Sara to speak. "No, I have not. You were my last person to call." He smirks again. He has completed the list. "Alright, I don't want to make you nervous or anything," Chris says casually. "I'll keep you posted. Okay, thank you. Bye."

"She lives around here?" Coonrod asks about

Sara.

"She lives in Aurora."

Downstairs, Nickolas speaks to his young sibling, who is losing patience with the situation now.

Chris and Coonrod talk about his career and how Chris suffered while working on cars with carpal tunnel symptoms. He explains how he used to work 8 days off and 6 days on, but now he works Monday through Friday and gets to spend more time with the kids.

They discuss Shanann's various medical conditions. Lupus, fibromyalgia, and rosacea, They thought she had Rheumatoid Arthritis. They discuss her list of medications: Imitrex for migraines, something for allergies, something for nausea.

Coonrod asks about medication changes and behavioral changes. They head downstairs and then outside the front door. Coonrod walks up to a slim man outside, dressed in light-colored pants and a maroon button-down shirt. "Tell them I will be there in just a minute," Coonrod instructs the group.

As the other officers head in the direction of the neighbor's house, the officer walks up to greet Dave Baumhover, the detective stepping out of the black SUV parked behind Coonrod's patrol vehicle.

Chapter 5

Nate the Neighbor

Officer Coonrod enters through the front door of the Watts' next-door neighbor's house at 2905 Saratoga Trail. The home-owner, Nate, is surrounded by Chris and Nickole in his large, vaulted family room. Coonrod walks up to the group as Nate, standing much taller than the others in an orange ball cap turned backward, and an oversize gray tee-shirt is positioned in front of his wall-mounted T.V. with his remote in hand, getting ready to show the officer what his footage reveals.

"What's that?" Coonrod asks Nate.

"Nothing' on there." Nate surmises as he speaks a command into his remote.

The woman on the tv advertisement closes her microwave door. Suddenly the image of Nate's driveway appears on the screen.

Chris starts listing off the things he loaded into his truck that morning, "I loaded my stuff up. My cooler, my water jugs, my book bag, my computers, some of the tools from the toolbox- I knew I was going to have to do some pumping in the rubbers today. That is why I was out so far." He types away rapidly on his phone.

"Is this on, continually recording?" the officer asks the homeowner. Chris looks up at Coonrod, licking his lips.

"Yup, yup. Well..."Nate begins.

"Is it motion?"

"Any motion events I've got." Nate clarifies. He scrolls through images on his surveillance video menu from different camera angles.

"But I get cars driving in from this street." He motions in the northwest direction with his left hand."This street." he points to the left as he motions west.

"This is him at 5:17."He states, pointing to the top of the screen. Chris frantically types into his cell phone. He turns to look. He sends a text message and turns his attention to the footage.

An image of Nate's truck parked in the driveway is depicted in the dark hours of the early morning.

He begins to narrate for his audience. "I usually park out there on the side." He points to the screen. "I just wanted to get everything back in. Be easier than lugging everything out there, all the tools I had to bring in."

He watches footage of himself on camera loading his truck up from merely hours ago. He takes a deep breath, looks toward the front door, and then turns back, resting his palms on top of his head with his fingers clasped, intertwined, and locked as if to keep his head from exploding. He takes a brief look at his cell phone as if waiting for a message that has not yet come through. He bites his bottom lip and begins rocking his weight from side to side.

He finds it more difficult to breathe as the adrenaline pumps through his veins and his body switches gears into extreme survival mode. He begins to breathe through his mouth. His limbic system is about to go into overdrive.

What did Chris see on the footage that completely set him off?

"What else can I do with this?" Chris licks his lips and peers at Coonrod through eyes wide and takes a deep breath.

"Um, my detective just showed up." Coonrod starts.

Chris rocks side to side.

"He'll probably want to talk to you. He probably, like I said he might have you call up the bank to see if there has been any, like, activity."

"Because if there was any sort of action out there," Nate interjects.

Chris raises his hand off the top of his head, which he had placed on his head like a hostage being led around.

"I would have got it," Nate promises.

"Under his camera - I had had an issue the other week," he points east. "People were stealing stuff out of, like, garages and stuff like that, and I had to park my truck."

Nate points on the screen, "I have you parked right here. So, I could see if anything happened." He points to the sidewalk east of his driveway.

"So, I could see if someone tried to jimmy with a flat head screwdriver." He is slouching as he scans the eyes of Nate and Coonrod for approval or threat.

"But if any action were to happen, any cars or anything that would have left your house," Nate reassures the young father.

"It would be right in that area. It should pick." Chris points to the top left corner of the screen, where his truck is clearly visible.

"Oh, it would pick up anything coming from down the street this way." He points west down Saratoga Trail.

"It would have been triggered back there?" Chris asks for clarification.

"Oh yeah! Watch, I'll show you."

Chris looks down and away. Nate continues, "There's nothing on here. We have already watched that one." He pulled up thumbnails of different videos taken from multiple angles. "At night, you'll see this car." He indicates footage of a gray sedan.

"How many security systems do you have?" Chris wonders aloud.

Nate answers, "Three. You can see this car is driving right down the street." The car was headed west to east as it approached Nate's driveway. "See, it picks up from all the way down there."

"That's cool." Chris is like a caged animal at this point, continuing to bite on the hair under his bottom lip.

"He's next door," Coonrod speaks into his radio.

Chris signals toward the front door. "You want me to go?"

"Talking to my dispatcher," Coonrod explains.

Chris looks down at his shoes.

"It'd be a code 4," Coonrod speaks into his radio. "We can pick up cars from this way and making a turn. I just pick up the cars pulling up to your." Nate's voice trails off. "So, unless they pull up right in here (he points to the area behind a tree that marks the space between their two driveways), but I would have caught her walking out."

Chris turns away again, scanning the front door exit. He slowly inches toward the door. He turns back around and bends at the waist.

"Nothing through the rest of the day?" Coonrod inquires.

"No, that's it." He turns off the surveillance footage. The image of a fetus in utero flashes on the TV screen. This was followed by an explosion and then a skull floating in oil.

"She's pregnant as well," Chris states as if he had forgotten.

"And how far along?'

"14-15 weeks. That's why her friend said it was low blood sugar." He pulls his phone back out.

Nate presses buttons on his remote. "You see, I've got her friend leaving out here at like two in the morning. My camera." His words, "My camera," suddenly appear on the screen.

The two men exchange words as the dog barks in the next room.

"Her phone was left here," Chris tells Nate.

"This starts recording at 1:48? And that was the start of the video?" asks the officer.

"Yes."

"It didn't pick her up going into the house, though?" Coonrod asks.

"It didn't, and I usually pick him up when he comes walking through here." Nate points to the part of Chris' driveway next to the front of the house. "So, it doesn't show her walking into the house. She would have walked by the way this is (pointed)." Nate decides. Chris signals affirmingly to Coonrod with his eyes. Chris feels around his jeans' pockets.

"How long does it typically record for?"

"30 seconds at least...at a time." Nate declares. "But this is at 1:48, and the next one I have is at 5 whatever," Nate explains. Chris nods. "No cars came through because, with the headlights, it picks up the headlights automatically."

"My Vivint said that at 5:27, my garage was left open." Chris begins. He pulls his phone back out again. "it says it was shut during the day. I think when Nicki's son, he may have tried to move the door around, maybe when they were trying to get in the garage door, and he probably broke the laser there. That's why my alarm started going off?"

"I know he said the front door he tried going in, but you had the lock-up, so that set it off." Coonrod corrects him.

"The remote on the outside doesn't work anymore. Got wet."

"Alright. Appreciate your time." Coonrod says.

Relieved, he shakes Nate's hand and looks straight into his eyes, "Thanks."

Chapter 6

The Armchair Detective

"My name is Alan, and I am the Armchair Detective." That is how I begin my shows on YouTube, Therefore, I'll do the same here to introduce myself to you in this book. When I am writing this chapter, it is the summer of 2021 in the United Kingdom. It has been nearly three years since this tragedy occurred, and I have spent countless hours delving into the details of this case.

I spend several hours a day broadcasting shows on three YouTube channels and Patreon. Just recently, I have surpassed over 80,000 subscribers and over 25 million views on my main channel. I also have a website and a Facebook Group where we can discuss the case further.

The first few chapters take you through the morning of August 13, 2018, from just after 5:15 am, when Chris Watts backs his truck up into the driveway, through roughly 2:45 pm, just before he is introduced to Detective Dave Baumhover. We have become acquainted with Chris Watts and several of the major characters as I have woven the dialogue from the police bodycam footage seamlessly with the discovery into a narrative with a high level of accuracy.

As the reader, you can visualize every moment as if you were standing beside Chris. I have taken hours listening to the words and utterances of everyone so that you will have the full dialogue, verbatim, and develop your own opinions about the case. I know my own theories have evolved tremendously over the past three years.

I have wanted to write this book for many reasons. The time and effort I have spent researching have brought to light several seemingly minute details of the case that, when considered in conjunction with everything I will present, will begin to paint a separate picture than what the official narrative depicts.

This case is one of the most heartbreaking cases I have ever seen due to how the bodies were disposed of, which is why this case garnered worldwide attention. The case is officially closed, but I do not think we have all the answers. They closed the case in record time, and I have made it my full-time job to analyze every aspect of this case in exquisite detail because law enforcement abruptly stopped the clock.

There is so much public information on this case that any true crime enthusiast, researcher, student, and even a regular Joe off the street has access to the police footage and discovery and Shanann's life on Facebook. Several books, documentaries made for TV movies, news reports, and interviews that all follow the same narrative.

These outlets have a large audience but stop short of positing new theories, perhaps fearing legal retribution. As opposed to the mainstream media, content creators' social media platforms, namely YouTube, have a license to freely express their opinions about what may have happened to Shanann and her children.

I believe it is now the time to bring our position to the mainstream. It's time that we, who have poured our hearts and souls into this case, earn the recognition we deserve by putting these revelations in print. I intend to lay it all out for you, in intricate detail, in one place. I have spent three years reviewing all the evidence and conducting my own investigations, and now, the time has come to report my findings to a broader audience.

We have chronicled the events and dialogue of the morning that Shanann and the girls went missing. There are several things I'd like to discuss that have occurred up until this point that needs mentioning. If I were Officer Coonrod, I might have noticed that Chris was wearing different clothes in the driveway footage than when he arrived for the wellness check. Certainly, if you accept that he committed these crimes in the timeframe he had available that morning, he would naturally have to change clothes and maybe shower to get rid of any trace evidence on his person.

There have been several discrepancies in his story so far. First, he tells Coonrod he left his house between 5:15 and 5:30 am. Later, he modifies that and says he left between 5:30 and 6:00 am. It may seem like a small detail, but a timeline discrepancy of just 45 minutes is significant when you consider all the tasks he would have carried out if you subscribed to the official narrative.

We now know exactly how long Chris spent loading up his truck until he drove away that morning, thanks to Nate's motion-activated home security systems recordings and the Geotab data from Chris' work truck. From the time he backed up his truck until the time he drove away, 28 minutes elapsed.

The District Attorney, in this case, Michael Rourke, would have you believe he spent this time loading the deceased bodies of his wife and two daughters into his truck, encased in black trash bags. However, if you look closely at the recording, you will not see Chris struggling to load anything heavy into either the bed or cab of his truck.

There is also the location where Chris parks his truck that morning. He parks on the road between his and Nate's driveways, but on this day, he parked further west down the street, totally obscured from camera view by what is affectionately known as the most hated tree in true crime. He never backs his truck into the driveway to load up his belongings before heading off to work.

This raises suspicion for the neighbor, as you will see, as we revisit that Monday in subsequent chapters. Chris is surprised when Nate reveals he has more than one camera that captures multiple angles outside of his home. He is also surprised to learn how far down the street the motion of vehicles can be detected activate those cameras. He becomes noticeably agitated at his revelation; we see it in his statements and body language.

There are also many discrepancies with his version of events as he relays information to Shanann's friends and family. We have Nickole at the helm driving the suspicion as she questions the flaws in his narrative. Namely, she is not satisfied with Chris's story about Shanann taking the girls on a play date. Nickole stated that Chris had originally told Addy that that Shanann and the girls left in the night, yet that detail is glossed over during questioning. So, we have three competing events here: Shannan took the girls on a play date, she went somewhere with friends, or she left with the children in the middle of the night.

Shanann's friends, family, and neighbors seem extremely concerned as they try to understand how Shanann could have left the house without detection. Meanwhile, Chris plays the part of the concerned husband as he sloppily provides contradicting statements. He is more concerned with gathering information about what the police might come to find out.

He does all this while delivering a narrative that makes no sense to investigators or loved ones. Why would Shanann leave without her car, phone, medications, handbag, or wedding ring? Chris never expresses any concern for his family. He only expresses concern that those around him are buying into his account of what happened.

He will continue to modify his statements over time, and we will see that nothing that Chris says can be trusted. We will detect a pattern in which he alters his story to fit any new evidence that surfaces. Why?

We are also left wondering who found Shanann's phone in the couch cushions that morning? It first appears on camera as Nickole and Chris try to work out the new passcode. Who found it? Was it Chris, or perhaps Nick?

Finally, I would like to leave you with arguably the most important fact that was glossed over during this line of questioning. "My Vivint said that at 5:27, my garage was left open. It says it was shut during the day." This quote from Chris Watts shows a nearly fatal flaw in Chris Watts's performance.

He left at approximately 5:46 that morning, according to the Geotab data released in the discovery documents. So, he leaves with the door inside his house to the garage open, and somehow it is closed during the day. He feebly tries to explain the Vivint alert as Nickole, but she sets off the alert at the front door at 12:10 pm, nearly 7 hours later.

Luckily, Coonrod shuts that theory down at the moment and is not fooled. Who shuts that door and when Chris is an hour away at the Cervi ranch?

These questions and more have arisen from the first nine hours of the investigation, from when he backs his truck up until Det. Baumhover arrives on the scene. There are a few moments of Nate's camera footage we have not yet scrutinized, just before Chris backs up into his driveway.

These will be some of the most hotly debated seconds of film associated with this investigation. We will look deeper into all those moments from 5:18 am until approximately 5:46 am, frame by frame for murder; seconds matter. Details matter. The truth matters. Justice matters.

Chapter 7

All I'm Saying

At 2:47 pm on August 13, 2018, Chris Watts walks out of his neighbor's house to meet Detective Dave Baumhover. He has just reviewed the footage of himself loading his truck that morning with his neighbor, Nate, and the responding officer. The first officer dispatched to the scene, Scott Coonrod, has called upon his detective to help investigate the possible whereabouts of Chris' pregnant wife, Shanann, and their two daughters, Bella and Celeste.

As Chris walks out the front door, Coonrod stays behind to get Nate's contact information. Nate immediately points out how oddly Chris is acting, rocking from side to side during the surveillance video review. They walk back over to the television, and Nate reveals how he never loads his stuff from the garage. He retrieves the driveway video on the screen.

"It doesn't look like he came from here (he points to the street between Chris' driveway and the neighbor's driveway on the west side) because he came from down the street." Nate decides, his eyes fixed on the screen. They watch as Chris' truck pulls up from the west and reverses into the driveway."And the other thing that doesn't make sense is why would you pull past this part?" He points to the part of the screen where Chris' garage begins. The tailgate of the truck is not visible on the screen.

"Are you able to record this?" Coonrod's requests.

"Uh-huh." Nate affirms."I'd have to call Comcast, but I can get them to do whatever. But watch you'll see him get out, and he walks back and forth a couple of times. To be completely honest with you, my wife and I wondered when she was on vacation if something happened because I have heard them screaming at each other at the top of their lungs. He gets crazy!"

"Does he?" Coonrod is intrigued. "That's pretty recent?"
"Yeah. I am guessing that's why she went and visited people because she wanted to get away from the situation."

Coonrod asks, "Do you have your I.D. on you?" Nates walks over to retrieve his wallet.

Nick walks in the front door. Nate speaks about how odd Chris recited all the items he loaded into his truck that morning because he is usually very quiet.

"What's your phone number?" Coonrod asks, and Nate obliges.

"It just seems kind of odd to me. Why would he pull the truck up into the garage?" Nate remarks.

"Right," Coonrod replies.

"Yeah. I have never seen him pull back." Nick says. "I've never seen him. If he loads his stuff, he normally just walks back and forth because I get him on camera, walking back and forth." Nate describes.

"What does he usually load up?" Coonrod inquires.

"All he usually has is a lunch box, and a bookbag looks like a computer, and usually a water jug. That's it." Nate recounts. "But the fact that he was in here explaining it over and over and over...He doesn't look worried. He looks like he is trying to cover his tracks. You know what I'm saying?"

"Right." Coonrod "...and if he's loading his stuff, why isn't he walking back and forth? But I can't see what he's doing in the back of the truck because he pulled into the garage. And he knows my camera is there."

"Any other neighbors around here have cameras you know of?"

"Um. I'm sure a bunch of them do, but not that I know of."

"I'll do a search here in a minute."

"All these tools come up missing, so when we moved in here, I put this in. And, as he said, someone was breaking into it. He said that someone was breaking into the toolbox of his truck, so I told him he could park his truck over here." He points to the street between their driveways.

Nickole comes in and mentions that Shanann's mom just texted, and there is GPS on his truck.

"I am just saying it's odd that he pulls his truck up back behind my camera," Nate says to Nicole. Nick nervously fidgets with the palms of his hands. The teenager is nearly as tall as Nate, with his mother's large brown eyes.

"The trucks in the garage, and he never backs his truck into the driveway."

"He carries his stuff into the house. He doesn't back his truck up!" Nickole proclaims.

"The other thing that's odd is that when she was gone, he kept parking his truck and her car over here (on the street) ...."

"He took the car out of the garage?" Nickole questions.

"The car was parked over there for a long time! "He points east."Like a couple of days."

"This past weekend?" Coonrod asks Nate.

Nick shakes his head.

"Um, no," Nate replies.

"It's when she was gone for six weeks." Nick clarifies.

"But I thought it was kind of odd that he never parked in front of here, or like here." He points west of the Watts' home. "He said someone broke into his truck!" He holds his fingers in quotation marks. "Hey, he's been acting so suspicious. He's normally- you can ask them- he's normally quiet, more subdued. He's over here telling me three times what he took out, what he did, he never talks. So, the fact that he's over here blabbing his mouth makes me suspicious."

Coonrod interjects, "Yeah, but I mean, put yourself in his situation."

"Oh, I agree."

"Anyone's going to be nervous. You don't know what to do."

"No, I agree, but I'm just saying the way he told you three times what he brought with him. Why is he telling you exactly what he brought with him instead of saying, 'Well, we didn't see anybody out here, didn't see anybody doing anything, you know what I'm saying? Why is he so worried about you knowing what he's carrying out? That's all I'm saying."

"The detectives talking to him," Nickole adds.

"He's talking to him right now. Okay." Coonrod walks toward the front door and exits the house.

Coonrod, Nate, Nickole, and Nick gather outside the Watts' garage and discuss which neighbors might have cameras. Nickole mentions she watched Shanann enter the home when she dropped her off early that morning. Coonrod notes that Nate's footage only detects her pulling away and not when she arrived.

Shanann's mother calls Nickole's phone and speaks to the officer. While he is on the phone listening to her, he looks in the trash can as he makes notes. He takes down her name and telephone number.

"How would you describe their relationship recently?"

Chapter 8

Detective Dave

Coonrod hangs up the phone with Shanann's mother, promising to provide her with updates as they come in. Just then, detective Dave Baumhover walks into the Watt's garage. Coonrod and Baumhover walk out of the garage for a brief chat. They walk back up to the garage where Chris Watts and Nate are standing behind Shanann's Lexus.

"Hey Chris, you okay if we just walk through and then look at her phone, if it's still up there?" Baumhover asks Chris.

"Yeah, yeah." Chris looks around the street and then back to the house. "I guess." He raises his eyebrows and walks the detective into the house from the garage. They walk past the formal dining room with a purple-painted ceiling and a play kitchen for the little girls and up the stairs. Chris unlocks the phone and hands it to the detective. Chris' gaze is fixed on the floor in front of him as he takes a deep breath.

'Do you have any current pictures of her?" Coonrod asks. Chris walks him into the master bedroom, in which the grand, four-poster bed with intricately carved leaves that spiral up to a wrought iron canopy is stripped of all its bedclothes. They walk up to the dresser, where family photos are placed below a wall-mounted flat-screen television.

"This trip is pretty recent?"

"That was last year," Chris replies, as Coonrod looks at a smiling photo of the couple from a cruise. Coonrod notices a pile of bedsheets crumpled up on the floor and begins to look through them. He shines a light on the bed, adorned with only the mattress protector.

"Code four." He calls into his dispatcher.

He begins snapping photos with his cell phone. Nickole and Baumhover enter and immediately look at the pile of laundry to the left of the door.

"Is this the suitcase she had?" the detective asks Nickole.

"No, it's downstairs,"

Nickole replies. Baumhover begins to go through the pile of bedsheets on the floor.

"I didn't see anything on those," Coonrod assures the detective. He walks into the master bathroom, shining his flashlight into the pristine bathroom sinks, then into the master closet. Shananns's favorite color was purple, and the word "Gorgeous" appears in decal on purple-painted walls above five black and white storage bins above color-coordinated racks of Shanann's blouses. The home is very well organized; aside from the vibrant favorite colors of Shanann painted on the walls in certain rooms, the home could be a model home for prospective buyers and is ready to show. They walk into the laundry room.

"There are clothes in the dryer." Coonrod relays. They continue the walk-through into Bella's room and then Celeste's, their names in cursive writing above each of their beds. The men comment on the Jack and Jill bathroom between the girls' rooms being locked on either side. Coonrod joins Baumhover and Watts, discussing the bank cards and identification found in Shanann's wallet.

Coonrod inquiries about the door between the girls' bedrooms, "What's this door right here go to? It's locked. Do you have a key for it?"

"Yeah, they wake up and play in the bathtub," Chris explains as he opens the door to the magenta- paint bathroom. "So, you normally keep it locked?" the investigators inquire.

"Yeah, because they'd be in the soap. The last time we had Vaseline everywhere. So, that was not fun." Chris justifies.

'So, does she normally make the kids' beds?" asks Baumhover.

"No," Chris responds.

"So, this all looks normal to you? Does this look like it was in a rush," Baumhover asks?

"No, they'll just go get her...." He raises his hands. "We don't wake up until they wake up." Chris places the key to the bathroom back on top of the door frame. They walk back into the loft area.

"Do you mind if I keep this and try and go through it?" Baumhover asks Chris about Shanann's phone. With his head cocked to the side and his hands on his hips, Chris stands, looking at Baumhover as the detective converses with the dispatcher. Coonrod converses with the dispatcher and makes his way downstairs as Chris and Baumhover discuss Facebook.

Coonrod makes his way downstairs and into the kitchen, whereupon the kitchen island resides a handbag. He answers a call from Sandra. Nickole walks up to Coonrod. "Is this her purse?" He asks Nickole.

"Is her medication - she takes these - her medication is still in here!" Nickole turns and walks a few steps back as the level of concern for her friend is heightened. She covers her face with her hands.

"We're going to get a hold of them. We're working on that," Coonrod assures the concerned mother of Shanann on the phone. Nickole turns back around and bites her lip, trying to make sense of everything. She furrows her brow and looks away in disgust. Nickole looks quickly at Coonrod on the phone with Shanann's mother and looks away with a heartbroken expression.

Coonrod reassures her mom, "Understandable, and we are doing everything we can to try and find her." Nickole grips her stomach and walks away as Coonrod snaps photos on his cell phone.

"I would know about that." Coonrod explains to her mom, "Possibly." Dieter, the Dachshund, cries from another room. "The beds are not made, no." He relays on the phone. The slender,salt-and pepper-haired detective and Chris walk into the kitchen.

Chris folds his hands across his chest as he gleans what he can from Coonrod's conversation with Shanann's mom. "We're going to try, alright," Coonrod promises her. "Yep...I will keep that in mind." Coonrod tells her, and they disconnect the call. Nickole looks on, disgusted. Chris looks at the phone, arms crossed.

Baumhover rests his hand on the kitchen island casually, yet his lips are pursed, and his eyes are fixed on the phone with curiosity and concern. He begins pacing back and forth. He walks off into the corner of the room and checks his phone, texting someone. Nickole begins biting her fingernails.

"I will keep that in mind, alright. Bye." Coonrod ends the call with Sandra.

"Did you tell your mother-in-law that she went to a friend today?" Coonrod asks Chris.

"Mmhmm," Chris replies casually, his arms still folded across his chest.

"Yeah? Whose. What friend?" Coonrod interrogates.

"Went to a friend's house. That's all I knew." Chris promises. The detective rests his body weight with his right hand on the kitchen island with his eyes staring at the marble counter.

"Who was she supposed to go to?"

"That's all she told me. She said she was going to a friend's house to take the kids."

"When was that?"

"This morning, she told me around 4, 5 O'clock." Chris' arms are folded, and he is looking down, defeated as if he has no confidence in his statement. He bites his bottom lip. Baumhover steps back, analyzing the situation, and is looking away from Chris, as if his assertions will add nothing of value to his investigation.

Coonrod walks up to the kitchen stove, whose clock reads 3:36. A brightly colored green kitchen towel hangs from the oven door handle, nearly the same shade as the kitchen walls. Chris and Baumhover exit. Coonrod asks Nickole,

"What were you guys saying about red on the stairwell. I didn't see what he's talking about."

Nickole points up the carpeted staircase. "There's red."Nickole points.

"No, I did a pretty good look everywhere, and I'm not...."He places both hands on the staircase at about waist-level. He takes a photo of a dark spot on the baseboard of the landing."It's a piece of wax or something. It's not blood. I don't see any signs of a struggle. Nothing's broken."

"What I don't understand is, like, her phone is her life." Nicole restates.

"Right, and her purse and her wallet., I mean the whole thing's...." Coonrod remarks.

"She never locks that door unless she's playing with the girls...and her shoes she orders a pair every year...."

"Those are the ones she normally wears. This is the suitcase she had yesterday?" He directs his attention to the suitcase next to the staircase.

Baumhover walks to the suitcase. "This is the stuff she had last night?" He asks Chris.

"Yep."

"What's this?"

"Uh, it's just some Anadarko stuff." "Is that your stuff?"

"That's some stuff I was going to give to people because they don't fit me anymore."

"All these are your jeans?" Baumhover lifts a pair of jeans and a bag next to the stairs.

"They're 38's, and they're way too big now." Chris checks his phone. He looks down at the bag of clothes for a moment as Baumhover loosens the collar of his shirt.

"Okay. Well, call anybody if you hear anything from her." Baumhover accepts his story about the clothes in the bag. "Just in case we need to trigger a missing person. I'm going to try and run things down using her phone and then see if we can't find somebody. Um, if nobody's heard anything at all, then we will probably pull the trigger a little bit quicker."

Nicole asks if they can start calling hospitals, and Baumhover says to go ahead, and he will try to canvas her friends. He suggests calling hospitals as well as hotels. Nickole says she has already called every friend of Shanann's. Chris checks both his work and personal cell phone.

"You want to talk before we go?" the detective asks.

"What about bank accounts, checking into that? We need account numbers or anything. Or have him call?" Coonrod suggests.

"That's why I was asking about the credit cards. None of your credit cards are missing either?" Baumhover asks Chris, and he shakes his head.
"Does she usually carry cash with her?" Coonrod asks.

"Not much, if any." Chris looks at the front door as if anticipating the moment everyone will leave.

"Well, there are some things we have to do before we do a flat-out missing person," Baumhover advises.

"So, if it does go to a missing person...I'm not sure how that works." Chris wants to know.

"What it would be is in the computer system, so if she pops up somewhere...Then on top with everybody looking around and asking around." He explains to Chris what will happen next as the group heads outside to leave.

Chapter 9

Consent to Search

Three uniformed officers, including Coonrod, Matthew, James, and Sargent Jared Bakes, conduct a search of the home. Chris signs the document at 4:36 pm. They advise that as the homeowner, he is free to be inside while they search.

Chris tells Coonrod, "Free reign, do whatever you got to do." They walk up to the front door as Dieter, the family dog, barks. "Let me get that dog out of here. He's going to flip."

The officers ask how long they have been married and whether this is unusual behavior for her. The step inside. Officer James asks what door they would normally use and asks about the ring doorbell camera. They ask if there have been any alerts, to which Chris replied, "Just when her friends were here."

"Does it only record when the doorbell rings? Or anytime someone...."

"If you're like right here." Chris walks out and stands on the cement walkway in front of the porch. "It should start; the proximity should hit up."

"Anything on that today?" James asks.

"Just her friends." "What time was that?"

"12:10. Ten minutes after noon." Chris stutters.

"Okay. Nothing in between the time when she got here this morning?"

"She got here at 2, yeah, 2 O'clock this morning. 1:48 on here. The only thing that was weird was the garage door, and it said it was left open after I left. It might have been the sensor, but my phone doesn't show, like, if it shuts." Chris explains.

"And who's your alarm through?"

"Vivint. But Nicki, her friend that came here at about 12:10, said the garage door was shut when she got here. That's the only thing that was weird." Chris decides to wait out on the front porch.

The officers begin a search of the home, beginning with the purse left on the kitchen island.

"Where's the purse at?" James asks Coonrod.

"On the counter." They walk up to the kitchen island.

"Whose phone is that?"

"I believe that is his; Baumhover took hers." Coonrod asserts while he sifts through the contents of her purse as James snaps photos with his cell phone. They comment on how "neat" the house is for having 2 little kids. They find Celeste's asthma inhaler in Shanann's office, remarking how Shanann did not take any of their medications. Unlike the rest of the house, the office is very disorganized, with piles of folders and documents and notes covering the top of her desk.

They split up and move on to different parts of the house. Coonrod feels the carpeting on the stairs while Officer James searches through the garage, closets, and basement. Coonrod comments on how organized the couple are as he makes his way up the steps, shining his flashlight through the carpet fibers along the way. He walks into the laundry room to the right of the master bedroom, shines a light on the clothes in the dryer.

He joins Bakes in the master, "I looked at the sheets and the comforters. I don't see anything. It's kind of odd nothing's on the bed, though…None of this was on here. We found it like this. He said when he left, she was in bed, sleeping." Coonrod begins turning over the pillows on the floor, looking for any evidence of foul play. In his report, he will later note that he found the fitted sheet next to the comforter on the floor and that the top sheet was not among the bedclothes in that pile.

"The only thing that's missing is the kids' blankies; they won't go anywhere without them," Coonrod says as they walk through the master bathroom and into the closet.

"So, they are gone?" Officer James asks.

"Yep. Car seats are in the car, and the keys are on the center console of the car. Cash, I.D. everything's...Phone's here." They continue to Bella's room and open the Jack and Jill bathroom door between the girls' bedrooms. Coonrod shines his flashlight through the corners of Celeste's room. The walls are painted a bright robin's egg blue with pink accents.

"There isn't any water in this toilet," remarks Coonrod.

"So, is she a stay-at-home mom?"

"She's a stay-at-home mom, but she works from home, and she does all her work through her phone. Her phone was on this couch, turned off." Coonrod clarifies as the three make their way through the upstairs.

"Did we go through the backyard at all? Can we?"

"I did not. I walked through there initially. I didn't see anything out of place. I was more focused on looking in, not at the yard." He recalls. The security bar on the sliding glass door prevented him from opening it earlier that afternoon.

They walk out through the sliding glass door to the back deck. Dieter the dachshund barks at the men.

"Yeah, I jumped down into the window wells, started looking through the windows, nothing. At first, they said she has diabetes, so I was thinking she was passed out." Coonrod begins. The men stand outside on the neatly trimmed lawn, looking toward a basement window.

Minnie Mouse looks back out at them from a sheet hanging on the window inside the basement. A toy shovel and rake are crossed in an "X" on the river rock beside the window well.

"Did he show up?"

"Yeah, he *finally* showed up because they had called him and said, 'Get your ass home.' So, I tried to get the garage door opener, and he said that didn't work. Said the button thing doesn't work. The garage door is pretty much shut down."

"So, he came home and let you in?" Bakes asks for clarification.

"He came home and let me in."

"What doesn't work, the garage door opener?" "He said the password on the outside, the code one doesn't work," Coonrod advises. "He closes it from the outside?'

"I don't know. It hasn't been closed since I've been here."

"The front door was locked, right?"

"I think he hit his garage door opener. The front door was locked."

"Was the deadbolt locked?"

"The top deadbolt, you can open it like 3 inches, then it locks. She had to go out of the garage because this door was closed and locked as a slider lock. So, she had to leave through the garage." Coonrod decides. "There's a house right on Steeple Rock that might have a good video, but they're not home.

"Right next door, he's got it, and it aims this way. It hits between their tree and the garage. So, at 5:27, Chris goes out, gets his truck, and backs into the driveway. He said he had to load up a bunch of tools. A neighbor said he never does that. Normally, he just grabs his backpack or whatever, walks out to the car, throws it in, and leaves. This morning he backs in, and it's on video at 5:27, but he backs, like, into the garage partially because you can't see the tailgate area. You can't see what he's loading. You don't see him loading anything. If you look into the back of his truck, it's still full of stuff. There's no room to put anything."

"Did we watch the rest of the video?" He asks Coonrod.

"Yeah. He watched it and said there was nothing. He said it's really good- it picks up any kind of car movement. But, at 1:48, when the R.P. drops her off, it doesn't pick her up pulling in. It doesn't see the wife getting out. It just shows her backing up and leaving. It's kind of choppy. I'm just trying to get more video."

Minutes later, as Coonrod continues searching the house, the other officer questions Chris about the pin pad outside the garage. They make their way out into the garage and look through Shanann's Lexus to see if her garage door opener is still on her visor. They open the hatch and see bags of clothes in the trunk.

Bakes and Watts make their formal introductions outside the garage. He asks about friends and family in the area and the bank accounts. Chris advises he has not checked the bank accounts yet but has checked with all her friends in the area. Bakes asks about any stockpiles of cash that might be in the house, to which he says not that he knows.

They walk out to Chris' work truck. The bed is packed with several large toolboxes, hoses, a tank, and some tools. Bakes calls dispatch to log the license plate on Chris' work truck.

Chris walks back into the house to get his credit card. James and Bakes discuss the truck's GPS capabilities. Inside, Coonrod asks Chris about the sheets being off the bed. Chris explains that Shanann must have stripped the bed after he left because she climbed right into bed when she got home from the airport.

Coonrod asks about the flip-flops by the door and if those are the shoes that Shanann normally wears, as Nickole asserted. Chris said she has a whole closet full of shoes. Coonrod asks again if he has any idea where his wife could be, and he says no. Meanwhile, Chris calls the bank.

"Do you know how many credit cards she actually has?" Asks Coonrod.

"Credit cards, no." He listens to Shanann's recent charges. "Taxicabs and limousines?" He looks up at Coonrod with a puzzled look on his face, offering, perhaps, a small morsel to the investigation. "The most recent one on the Chase is a taxicab and limousine company for $15.32."

"When was that?" "August 12."

"Did they say where?"

"No. They said a merchant known as Taxicabs and Limousines." He continues listening to the recent transactions.

"August 13. 27 bucks at Target." he offers Coonrod.

"Which credit card is this?" interrogates Coonrod.

"USAA," answers Chris.

"It's the same account? It's probably pulling out of your account; the purchase was probably a couple of days ago then." He concludes, not taking the bait.

They join the other two officers and discuss the recent purchases and whether Shanann and the girls have passports. Chris is unclear about exactly how many credit cards she has. They discuss the medications they take and the timeline of events. Chris mentions a birthday party he took the kids to the previous day at a friend's house down the street while they were in his care over the weekend.

James asks if someone is sleeping in the basement. Chris says he has a few times due to the separation. He says the last time he slept in the basement was probably Thursday or Friday night. He asks if the children sleep in their own beds, to which Chris confirmed that they do. Bakes asks about the bedsheets in the master bedroom.

He explains that she went to bed immediately when she got home from her trip to Arizona and that usually, she would wash the sheets immediately to 'get the airport off them.' He asks Chris if he slept in the master bedroom the previous night, and Chris says he did to watch the baby monitors while waiting for Shanann to get home from her trip. Officer James asks if she ever goes on walks, to which he replies she doesn't, but he jokes for runs.

"What was the conversation this morning you guys had?"

"It was about us selling the house and the separation."

"How did she take that?"

"We were *both* pretty emotional, both crying." Chris answers.

"And then did you see her before you went to work? Did you say anything to her?"

"Mmm. She went back- she told me she was going to go to a friend's house and be with the kids- take the kids with her."

"Oh, she told you she was taking the kids." "Yeah. Yeah." He raises his eyebrows.
"She didn't say who, though? James asked.

"Oh no. But she was still in bed when that happened." Chris is sure to mention.

"And this was after the conversation?" questions Bakes.

"This was between like 4 and 5 am. I woke up about 4 O'clock."

"What time did she get home?"

"1:48," Chris says confidently, reciting data from his ring doorbell camera.

"Did you guys sleep for a while?"

Chris raises his eyebrows again. "Oh yeah, I was, like, passed out when she got home."

"And did you wake her up?" "Yeah, when I got up."

"And that's when you discussed the issues?" Bakes continues.

"Yeah. I didn't want to do it over a text or a phone call. I wanted it to be face-to-face with her." He says, with a distinct glottal fry.

"How long did that conversation last?"

"Probably like 30-45 minutes." He slightly raises the corners of his mouth, and his eyes flutter rapidly.

"And then you went to work?"

"Mhmm, I left about 5:15, 5:30. In that time frame."
"And she said she was going to a friend's house with the kids."

"Mhmm, she was still here when I left." He moistens his lips and briefly looks up and to the right as he delivers his answer.

"You went to a job site or the main plant, or where did you go?" Coonrod stands with his right arm across his chest and his left hand on his chin, partially covering his mouth.

"I went to the location first." "Where's that?"

"By Hudson. Over there, east of Hudson."

"And there was someone there the time you got there?"

"No, no. No, one of the other operators had an issue there on Friday. Nothing runs over the weekend. I went over there just to kind of verify what kind of issue he was- he was having, see if I could fix it." He nods his head. "Then we went to a pumping unit, across the- across the ranch over there. I was there most of the day, and that's when I got the phone calls and text messages and came home."

"Were you guys on like County Road 49, or where were you guys at?" James asks him. Chris turns to face James and sucks in his bottom lip.

"Oh, like, you know where, like, Roggen is?" "Yeah," James responds.

"Yeah, out there."He says with a low, creaking voice.

"Whose ranch were you on?" "Cervi," Chris says quietly.

"Okay, I know where that's at," James tells him.
"So, what kind of tools did you have to load up in the garage?"

"It was just mainly, I got my water bottles, my water jug, my computer, bookbags and my containers full of... just my O rings, all that stuff. Just putting all of that stuff in there because I took it all out." Chris stutters through an explanation of how his tools went missing because he left his truck unlocked. He explains how he put all his tools back after being in the garage over the weekend.

They tell Chris that if he talks to Shanann, please reach out to the police so they know she is okay. They exchange contact information, and Chris walks them out the front door.

Chapter 10

Monday Evening

After the police left that evening, Chris found himself all alone in an empty house. Earlier that afternoon, Chris received a call from his friend, Nick, stating that he and his wife, Amanda, had just arrived home from a Kentucky trip. He asked Chris when he could go for a run, as he was training for a big run the following month. Chris responded, breaking the news that Shanann and the girls were missing, that he hadn't heard from them all day, and that the cops were there. Nick asks Chris if there is anything they can do, offers to head over to Chris' house, bring him some food, and let him know that they were there for him.

Nick and Amanda arrive that evening sometime between 6:00 and 6:30 and greet Chris at the door. He goes on to explain the situation, that he and Shanann had been having marital issues, about the emotional conversation the two had had that morning before Chris went off to work, and how Shanann had essentially disappeared with the girls. Chris tells Nick and Amanda that he was at work when he received texts from Nickole that Shanann wasn't responding to calls or text messages and that she was at their house.

Chris tells Nick that on the way home from the job site, he calls the girl's school and asks if they had been there that morning, and finds out that they hadn't checked in, and asks them to keep the girls on the waitlist. In actuality, he had called Primrose just before 8:30 that morning.

He tells the couple that the cops were there when he arrived, did a walk-through, and returned with a search warrant. They continue talking at the kitchen table about the cops taking Shanann's phone, the neighbors' security footage, and the taxicab charge on their credit card.

Chris tells Nick that he was in the process of contacting the local hospitals when they arrived. To Nick, Chris seemed lost, just trying to process everything. He confided to Nick that he was worried about speaking to the news media and being looked at as the prime suspect. Amanda offered to have Chris spend the night at their house, but Chris declined, saying he would spend the next night.

Lauren, one of Shanann's childhood friends who lived in the area, saw a Facebook post from Shanann's younger brother that Shanann, Bella, and Celeste were missing. She had tried to get in touch with Shanann earlier that day to see how the doctor's appointment went for the baby, with no reply from Shanann. She did not have Chris' number, so she decided to show up at their house to see if she could find out more.

When Lauren arrived, Nick and Amanda were there with Chris. He hugged her by the front door, and she noticed the flip flops Shanann always wore were by the front door. She also noticed Shanann's suitcase, still packed, next to the bottom of the staircase. She also saw the kid's toys in the living room, which seemed strange to her.

Shanann always kept the house tidy, and the toys there seemed out of place. She glanced up the stairs, and Chris immediately commented that he had to close all the doors upstairs because he did not want to see the kids' toys. This made Lauren wonder why the toys on the lower level scattered about the living room did not seem to bother him.

Lauren asked Chris if he had driven around looking for Shanann, and Nick answered that the police advised him not to. She asked again, and again, Nick answered that the police said it was not advisable. As she was talking to Chris, she scanned his arms for any signs of injuries. She also noticed that anytime she would ask Chris about Shanann and the girls, he would avoid eye contact and look down at the floor.

Lauren thought that Chris did not seem concerned about Shanann or the children. He seemed to be confused and not altogether present in the moment. She asked whether Chris had planned to go to work the next morning, and he said he would try and go in because he didn't want to be in the house and didn't know where else to go.

Lauren left about a half-hour after arriving and decided to drive through the neighborhood to see if she could find any signs of her missing friend and the girls. Nick and his wife also left around 8 O'clock that evening.

Not long after they left, another friend of Chris' named David receives a message from a mutual friend named Jeremy, who had previously worked at a Ford dealership with Colon, Chris, and Shanann. Colon also lived in the Wyndham Hills subdivision and had received a text message from Jeremy asking what was going on with Chris and Shanann.

Jeremy had seen a post on Facebook from Shanann's mother that Shanann and the girls were missing. He read the post several times because he was in disbelief. Chris had just been at his house the previous day for a birthday party for his young son, and his daughter had just been at the Watts home babysitting for the girls the day before that. He decided to text David to see if he could check on Chris.

David walked over to the Watts home, arriving around 9:30 pm after speaking with Chris on the telephone. When he arrived, Chris had been keeping himself busy with housework, and he could see the lines had recently vacuumed the floor on the carpet. He joined Chris in the kitchen, where Chris was preparing a protein shake, and the two talked about the situation with Shanann and the girls.

Chris told Colon that Shanann had taken off. When asked about surveillance videos, Chris said he had none and that the neighbors had none. A few minutes later, Chris received a phone call from who he said was his mom, saying that everyone on Facebook was suspecting Chris had been involved with their disappearance. Shortly after, Jeremy arrives, and the men talk for about 15 minutes or so before Chris tells them he needs to lie down, and they leave around 10:15 that evening.

As it turns out, Chris did not receive a call from his mother that evening. It was from someone else who seemed very concerned that Chris was under suspicion on social media. Chris had received a call at 9:48 pm that evening that lasted until 10:38, about half an hour after Jeremy and David had left for the evening. Did Chris keep the line open during his visit with Jeremy and David? Was the call on speakerphone for the person on the other end to hear the conversations in the house that night?

Pictures

Chris sees something on the TV screen that makes him panic.

Chris greets Law Enforcement at the door and gives
consent for the K9 units.

Thursday, August 16, 2018, ~ This is where Shanann's body
was buried in a shallow grave.

This is the sheet found out in the field approx. 80 feet from the shallow grave.

Chris signed and dated this aerial photo of Cervi 319
showing where he marked S, B, and C.

An unidentified person walking out of the garage

A clip from my video showing how the shadow and Chris
came together in the CCTV footage.

NO shadow is seen under the truck.

Shadow IS visible under the truck.

Chapter 11

Follow the Scent

Search and Rescue dogs of the United States (SARDUS) arrived on the scene Tuesday, August 14, 2018, shortly after the missing person's report had been filed. The pace of the investigation into the disappearance of Shanann and the girls was rapidly accelerating, and the Frederick Police had enlisted the help of the CBI and FBI.

At roughly 2:00 am, Officer Ed Goodman tried to contact Chris to inquire about the girls' height, weight, eye, and hair color for the missing person's report. When he attempted to call Watts' personal cell phone, there was just dead air, so he tried multiple times to no avail.

Watts called him back a few minutes later from his work phone, stating that something was wrong with his personal cell phone. It struck Goodman that Chris did not ask if he was calling to report any new developments or found his wife and children.

Around 11:45 am representatives from the Frederick Police Department and Boulder County Sheriff's department, along with Sardis, arrived at the Watts home to conduct another search, to which Christopher Watts gave his consent. A news crew was set up on the sidewalk interviewing Nickole Atkinson on the sidewalk in front of the neighbor Bette's house when they approached the home.

The officers were shown into the home, and they looked for personal items belonging to Shanann and the girls. Chris stated that his dirty clothes were mixed with Shanann's, so Shanann's shoes were used for the dogs to collect the scent. The girls' shoes from the day of the birthday party were collected. Deputy Katherine Tkach assured Chris that they would do everything they could to find his family for him.

When they entered the house, it was clear that Chris was busy cleaning as the strong scent of cleaning chemicals hit the searchers. David had noticed the night before, and there were also fresh lines on the carpet from the vacuum cleaner. To the officers, Chris was emotionless, unless he smirked or smiled inappropriately and showed no empathy. His emotions didn't even change when speaking of his little girls, who had now been missing for over 24 hours.

Chris was asked to remain outside, so there was no interference with the dogs. Jayne Zmijewski explained that the dog she was handling, Kodi, a Chocolate lab, was a cadaver dog and would alert areas where there had been trauma or a struggle. Officer Katherine Lines escorted Jayne and Kodi as they made their way around the home. Immediately when they walk into Bella's room, Kodi starts barking, alerting them to the area underneath Bella's bed. Officer Lines climbs down to look and notices a children's book, All by Myself of the Little Critter Series, as well as a rock.

Jayne decides that was what the dog was showing her, stating the scent of the body will fall. Officer Lines walks back into the laundry room and begins taking photos of the girls' clothing from the laundry hamper.

Jayne calls Lines into the girl's bathroom, where she notices sediment in the commode. She comments on the layers of sediment, and no water is in the toilet. Officer Lines opens the lid in the tank revealing water, to which Jayne remarks, "That's kind of weird."

"It almost seems like this place is a little bit too immaculate to be normal," Jayne remarks.

"It's amazingly clean!" Lines agrees. "You know what I'm saying, though? I do."

They go through CeCe's room and into the loft, where the dog begins barking in the southwest corner of the room. They move right past the bathroom to the left of the playroom as the dog shows no interest in that area. They move to the brightly colored playroom, adorned with shelves lined with books, a toy kitchen, and a Papasan chair, seated with two "My Size" articulated dolls.

The dog barks again. They go into the master bedroom, where the bed is still stripped of the bedsheets. The dog barks, again, just twice.

Lines receives a call on her phone from Officer Ivan Perez and meets him at the front door. She explains that the dogs outside are the other track team, that Jayne's dog, Kodi, is looking more for "trauma and heated areas," whereas the other teams outside the door are looking more for the scent.

Lines rejoins Jayne, and they head downstairs into the basement. Jayne asks if the other teams have started yet, and she indicates that they have not. When they get downstairs, Lines notices a plastic storage bin on a shelf filled with Albuterol and other medications.

"That's interesting," she comments as she snaps a few photos—Kodi barks once as Jayne opens the door to a black refrigerator. Jayne moves over to a group of suitcases underneath a window. Kodi whimpers. Lines decides to turn and have another look at the prescription bin as Kodi starts barking and whimpering near a home gym area located in front of a window, covered by a pink sheet featuring Minnie Mouse waving and smiling. The chime of the motion sensor startles Jayne, and she looks up at the rafters.

Jayne opens the cabinet door located under the basement stairs, and Kodi barks very loudly and intently.

"Are you trying to tell me something?" she asks her canine companion. Kodi continues to bark and pant. "Something's upsetting him here." She tells Lines.

"Hmm." Lines remarks, typing into her phone.

"Something's upsetting him here, in this area," Jayne repeats. "Mark this area here as an area of interest."

Jayne continues, "His nose is down to the ground a lot over here; you notice that?"

"Mhmm."

"And it's been up in the air." Kodi continues barking.

"Will the furnace affect any of that?" questions Lines.

"Well."Jayne considers that possibility. "Do I need to shut it off?"

"There's a fan in there." Lines reached behind the furnace and flipped off the switch. They move over to an area with an unmade bed. Kodi continues to bark fervently.

"I think Jeff or one of the others should come down in here," Jayne recommends.

" This bed is definitely not made. Stuff on hangers, coats...." Lines observed.

"That intensity." Jayne begins, "See, he hasn't been that intensity."

"There's a dead wasp on the bed. There's a sleeping mask there, too." Lines shines her flashlight on the bed, and Jayne steps over to look.

"This has not been cleaned up like everything else."

"Sure hasn't." Lines replies.

"See, this may be her scent."Jayne looks Lines directly in the eyes, "Something has set him off."

"Maybe get Jeff or one of the others in here and see. Because with this...." Jayne insists again.

"I'll have officer Perez send one of them in."

"Before they get going, just have him bring them down into this area and see."

Kodi continues to bark. "Okay, that's a good boy. Come here. Sit down. That fan going?" I just shut it off."

"Hard to tell where that scent's actually coming from."

"Yeah, for sure." Lines calls Perez, "Hey, can you send one of the K9s down to the basement, please? Yep, she's going to take her dog out, and we need to have one of them come in, and I'm going to stay in the basement and wait for them. So, she's coming out right now. Uh, big time, but we don't know what, so that's why we're going to have one of the others come in.

They have different- different skill sets. So, keep everybody out. She's coming out and has another K9 come in. Alright?Okay." Lines ends the call. Jayne goes back upstairs, and she shines her flashlight under the basement steps and near the gym equipment next to the Minnie mouse window, searching for any clues as to why the dog would be alerting so intently in these areas.

A few moments later, another handler comes down with a second dog, not on a leash. The dog sniffs the bed and around the basement and is quiet, compared to Kodi. This dog seems to have been trained to give passive indications for an alert.

"Dex, come here." The handler motions to a basement area just behind the cabinets under the stairs that Kodi had alerted to stacked with storage bins containing holiday decorations.

"Do you need a flashlight?" Lines asks.

"So, he's not doing his trained final alert...I'd say there's a little interest here. Dex, come here, please. It may be worth looking at this mat if things develop." He shines the flashlight on his phone on a rolled-up yoga mat. "It's just kind of... I don't know. It's just kind of- had a little bit of... Is this where Jayne's dog had interest too?"

"Um, the opposite side." She shines her flashlight through the spaces between the storage bins to the area beneath the stairs where Jayne's dog gave an active indication.

"So, the bed area, and we actually shut off the furnace, just to eliminate that." She moves her hand in a rotating gesture. "From the other direction, right where those coolers were. So, just a lot of refocusing, refocus, refocus. So, I don't know."

"So, if there were a body, there would be a lot of interest."

"Am I good to turn this back on?" She asks about the furnace fan. They walk around to the other side.

"So, it was just a lot of revisiting right here. The only thing, there's a bag of rope and some tie-downs and a whole bunch of paint cans." Lines shines her flashlight around the area.

"So, I am pretty confident there would not be a body or parts." He walks around to the shelves with the prescription container. "It's very organized."

"Yes, it's very organized, very clean. I mean, there's not even dust in the basement." remarks Lines.

They walk up the stairs, and the handler asks Lines if Jayne had searched the garage, to which she replies, no. They plan to go out to the garage and then outside the house.

In the garage, the dog goes around the Lexus without incident. Lines asks if he thinks the house is clear of death at this point, but he continues to go around. The chime of the motion sensor finally goes off, over a full minute after they enter the garage. They head through the house, completely bypassing the additional search of the second floor since Jayne's dog did not indicate any trauma or death upstairs.

They walk out the front door where Chris is standing on the porch with Tom Koppough setting up for their interview, and she indicates it's okay for Chris to go inside.

"That's okay." Chris shrugs with shallow energy. Lines walks up to Perez and says they are done inside the house. Lines checked with the team and told Perez they were done with the house and did not need to go back in.

Nearly an hour goes by, and Lines accompanies Jane on a foot search of the neighborhood. Kodi starts a frenzied alert just as Jeff's daughter runs up to Jayne and says that her dad needs to speak with her urgently. Jayne trades the leash for the phone and walks off to speak to him, away from Kodi, whose barking rings like thunder in her ears.

Now Kodi, the search dog, and the rescue dog are in his element. He is wearing a bell that rings to notify Jane of his location, just like he would if he were searching in the wide-open spaces of Colorado. Many houses in that neighborhood area are still under construction, and portable restrooms line the streets for construction crew members working their various trades.

One such worker is on a ladder working on the home's gutters located at 6229 Marble Mill Place. All the top windows of the house are open to let the breeze in on this hot August afternoon.

Kodi looks to his handler, squealing and howling for her to return. He is running around, trying to get the attention of Jeff's daughter and Officer Lines, the pitch of his barking rises.

A moment later, she returns at a hurried pace, sensing his distress. She hands the phone back and walks up to Lines. She looks in the direction of the worker standing on the ladder, "I know what he's doing. Jeff said the scent from the house is over here, so that's exactly what he's doing. He's picking up the scent from the house."

They walk across the empty lot and between two houses, then head north on Black Mesa Drive, crossing Sterling Court, to an empty field, enclosed by red netting, that surrounds the Wyndham Hills clubhouse. Kodi barks again and continues to lead the way.

"When he stops, I'm going to stop," Jayne announces. Kodi stops halfway down the field where Waterman Way meets Black Mesa Drive, discouraged by the netting that blocks his intended path.

Lines responds to the dispatcher, "989: Code 4, no need," indicating that the scene is safe and no assistance is needed. He barks and turns to Jayne, then starts heading northeast toward Emerald Drive across the field. They stop to look into a container, and then Lines mentions the ground has not been disrupted.

"Winds changed," Jane notes aloud. They cross the street and stop in front of 2612 Emerald Drive.

"Calm down, just a little bit," Jayne instructs Kodi as he begins to bark. Jayne bends down to give him some water. "Storm is forming, that wind is...we hardly don't have a predominant wind anymore. I've run out of water; we'll watch for a hose attached to one of these houses."

Jane suggests heading back south since Jeff is headed north with his companions before heading back to the house. They continue walking toward a vast open area near the northwest corner of Black Mesa and Steeple Rock Drive, then start heading across the open area toward an oil pump.

"Would he have had time to go bury somebody?" Jayne asks Lines.

They trek on until they get to the corner of Goldfields and Black Mesa, where they happen upon something that catches Lines' attention. She stops to pick up a cartridge shell with a black glove. Jayne decides it's most likely a 17 caliber round. They notice two more, along with a 10 round cylinder side plate. Jayne asks if there is a firing pin mark, and after inspection of one of the rounds, Lines determines it is closed and has not been fired.

They head back toward the direction of the Watts' house. Lines asks Jayne if the dogs could not pick up a scent if that would indicate that she left in a vehicle on the property. Janes says that it would, or perhaps a vehicle sitting out on the road.

"And then at what point would the dogs be able to follow that scent?" Lines asks. Jayne advises that it would be difficult because the scent would mingle with the scents of others in the vehicle, and although possible to trail a vehicle, it would be difficult in the time frame since the disappearance.

I believe that the dogs alone proved at this moment that no one died in the house.

Chapter 12

Bombshell Witness

The storm clouds rolled in over the Denver area on the evening of August 14, 2018. Shanann Watts and her two girls were still missing. Teams of investigators were working tirelessly to fit the pieces of this puzzle together to find out what happened to this vibrant and captivating woman and her precious daughters.

She had what most would consider the perfect life; two adorable children with a third on the way, a beautiful home, a successful career, and a doting husband, or so it seemed. It is hard to imagine who would want to harm this woman and her children, but on this evening, the fingers were all aimed at one person: Christopher Watts, her husband of nearly six years, best friend, and father to those innocent children.

They say that no marriage is perfect, but to those looking on from social media, most friends, co-workers, and neighbors, Shanann and Chris came as close to perfect as you could probably get. However, some were close to Shanann, like Nickole, Cassie, Addy, the neighbor Nate, and others, who started to see the cracks in the foundation of this marriage shortly before the disappearance. It was people like these who are the heroes in this story and sounded the alarm early. It is also the law enforcement officers who are heroes; they acted quickly and did their best to bring their own part of the puzzle forward, and once they brought their pieces forth, they were no longer in their hands, and they had no control over how the puzzle was put together.

Close friends and family members had intimate knowledge of how Chris had been behaving toward Shanann; he was distant, no longer the doting husband and father who would reluctantly appear in the posts on social media for Shanann's business.

Family members of Shanann would recall this change in Chris during his visit to North Carolina just weeks before. Shanann was very sick on the first evening that Chris was there, and instead of caring for her through the night as he normally would have done, he slept out on the couch, and it was her younger brother who looked after her. Shanann knew something was different, and she confided with close friends her suspicions as to why.

On August 14, at 8:07 am, Investigative Analyst Ganley of CBI received information from Agent Galbraith that Chris Watts possibly had a girlfriend. This information was forwarded by Tony from Anadarko Petroleum Corporation, who thought the information might be relevant, and Agent Galbraith wanted a full workup of the possible girlfriend, which was provided to all relevant parties in law enforcement.

Later that day, Ganley received the cell phone return from Verizon Wireless for Nichol Kessinger and started building a timeline in an analyst notebook with the data from the cell phones and official police reports. On September 11, 2018, another investigation was determined to complete the timeline, and Analyst Ganley's work on the timeline ceased.

Nichol Kessinger was a contracted employee of Anadarko who reportedly worked for Tasman GeoSciences, whose job responsibilities included Quality Control/ Safety and helping to survey land, as reported in the discovery document released by Weld County.

She started working with Christopher Watts sometime around April 2018, although this could not be independently confirmed. She reportedly came to law enforcement of her own volition to reveal the nature of her relationship with Christopher Lee Watts, and again, this information could not be independently confirmed.

Nichol Kessinger was first interviewed on August 15th at Majestic View Nature Center by Special Agent Phillip Jones. Her father accompanied her during this interview. The subsequent interviews were conducted by CBI agent Kevin Koback, beginning on August 16th at the Thornton Police Department. Then another interview onAugust 17th via telephone and on August 21st via telephone. Her final interview was on August 23rd at the CBI office in Lakewood, Colorado. She did meet with Koback a final time on September 4, at the CBI in Lakewood, where he introduced Dave Baumhover as her point of contact going forward.

She deleted all text messages from Chris Watts. Two attempts were made to recover the information from Kessinger's iPhone 6, first using XRY software, then using Cellebrite software, with her consent. She transferred her phone service to an older Samsung S5 and recovered multiple previously deleted text messages.

With regards to the cell phone data extractions, "logical" data extractions were conducted at the Northern Colorado Forensic Laboratory, but at the time of the investigation, it was reported that they did not have the technology to conduct a "physical" extraction from Apple devices, which would include deleted or hidden data, but is also more difficult and time-consuming. There are 7 screenshots of text messages between Chris Watts and Kessinger available in the redacted discovery files available at the time of publication. These messages were obtained from Watts' phone, presumably because Kessinger reported the sim card from her phone was broken. It is worth noting that the multiple text messages recovered from her phone were not in the Weld County discovery document.

In addition to the text messages mentioned above, there were also text messages between Kessinger and Koback referenced. Of those, there were a total of four text message screenshots provided to Koback by Kessinger redacted from the discovery document originally released. These four screenshots were among the seven in the redacted final document.

There was a search warrant issued and executed for the phones of Watts and Kessinger. The data from the phone dumps from those phones were checked in on 10/2/2018 and is stored on a 4-terabyte external hard drive in an evidence locker at Frederick Police Department.

Chris Watts had a secret calculator app on his personal cell phone to which he transferred data from his phone starting in the middle of July, presumably to hide evidence of his affair from his wife. This app is capable of storing photos, videos, contacts and even has a private browser.

This data contained images that were not included in the 50-page Cellebrite report. According to the analyst, although a warrant was sought, it is unclear if a search warrant was issued or executed for this information from the secret calculator app. The 50-page report is in chronological order with notes from the analyst and is found in the redacted final discovery document.

It is obvious from the Cellebrite report that Watts and Kessinger were having an affair. The first phone call between Watts and Kessinger is reported on July 7, 2018 (also the day that Shanann left for North Carolina with the girls), although one screenshot of the text messages retrieved from Watts's phone indicate that they were involved on June 27 and are as follows and are presumed to be from Watts to Kessinger based on the content:

"Promise! I'm about loyalty, truthfulness, and being dedicated. I don't like playing games... unless it's role-playing {Wink face emoji}

"If you want me there, I will be there! Ice cream, cookies, and lollipops...sounds like a cheat meal night lol" -sent 6/27/18 2:42 PM. "

I'm still going to see you! It won't be as often as we like, but I will make it happen. Do you think you're the only one addicted right now? I'm so hooked on you."

-sent 6/29/187:34 PM

"Sleeping without your warm body next to me isn't going to be fun tonight" -sent 6/29/18 8:12 PM.

From the context of the messages, it stands to reason that their relationship had been ongoing for a much longer period of time at this point, from phrases such as "as often as we like" and "sleeping without your warm body next to me." It is reported that their relationship only lasted 6 weeks, but in my opinion, it was going on for much longer.

The Cellebrite report also contains the web searches Shanann, Chris, and Kessinger made on their phones. The first entry on page one of the Cellebrite report is dated *September 1, 2017,* and it is of a search made by Nichol Kessinger for the name "Shanann Watts."

The five interviews of Kessinger reveal a lot of information about their relationship and possible insight into what may have been going through Watt's mind from a very intimate source. Although this book chronicles only the first two days of the investigation in narrative form from the video recordings, from the time Nate's security footage begins recording at 5:18 am on August 13 through the end of the recording on agent Lines body cam video during the K9 searches at 2:26 PM on August 14, it is important to point out some things from those interviews based on the interview notes for contextual purposes.

These notes are summarized and are not verbatim, and the statements below are from her perspective based on conversations she allegedly had with Watts. Apart from the first interview, the subsequent interviews were conducted after Chris Watts confessed to the murders of his wife and children, and it is presumed from the context of the second interview that Nichol was aware of his confession.

There are no interview notes in the redacted final discovery document from the first interview with the FBI on August 15. The report page indicates that the document is property of the FBI and that the FBI retains ownership of the document. It is largely just a description of the property evidence regarding the audio recording that was collected during the investigation.

This interview was conducted under the supervision of her father, although he is not named in the document. This was conducted on the same day the email was forwarded from Anadarko that alerted the CBI of her involvement with Chris Watts.

It is unclear from the discovery when and how the mistress allegedly came forward of her own volition. Still, it stands to reason that it was after that email was received, based on a statement from the notes on her August 16 Interview that states: "Nichol spoke with her father about the situation, and they decided to come to the police. She said she wished she had come in earlier, but it took her *a few days* to process what was going on."

The second interview was the only one that was video recorded. She had asked for a ride to the Thornton Police from agents Koback and Martinez, and they picked her up *near* her home in Northglenn. Her father accompanied her to the interview but drove himself. He was not present during the interview as he was on the previous day. The only details from this interview were the words:

"Recorded interview of Nichol Kessinger[PROTECT IDEN-TITY] on August 15, 2018."

Before this, she had given Chris the benefit of the doubt, and murder was never in her mind. She thought that Shanann had just left. She met him in early June or May *at work,* and she did not mention he was in a relationship or had children and was not wearing a wedding ring. One day, he mentioned that he had children, and she thought it was "cute."He mentioned he did have a significant other, but they were in the process of separation. Their first meeting outside of work was at the end of June or the beginning of July.

They had a lot in common, like fitness and cars. He was willing to "learn new stuff" and interested in what she had to share with him. They spent all their time dating either at her place, or they went out, but she had *briefly* been to his house twice; once on July 4, where she helped him set up fitness apps, and he cooked lunch for her, and once on July 14, where she saw a picture of his wife and "one of his kids," and she encouraged him to work things out with his wife.

She did not like being there because she respected that like *their* space. She doesn't know the street name of his address. He went to North Carolina to try to fix things with his wife, and she thought their relationship would be over at that point.

She felt bad about not waiting until he was divorced completely before starting a relationship with him. She never met his children. She learned Shanann was pregnant from newspaper articles on Monday and Tuesday, which made her think his wife may be in danger. If she had known Shanann was pregnant, she never would have wasted her time on him.

She has two phones, and they first communicated via her work phone. Her employer pays for her work phone, but it belongs to her, and she does personal stuff on it. She deleted all Chris' Watts' information from his phone because she was hurt and grossed out by him. She has no social media accounts. She met with her dad Wednesday, and they decided to go to the police.

She cut him off after talking to him Tuesday, and he was a hot mess. He lived in the basement, and he was always in the basement when they talked. Chris was trying to save his marriage, but Shanann didn't want it. Shanann had bad spending habits, and they were "house broke." He told her they made about the same amount of money.

Chris never told her where his kids went to school. They first went to the Lazy Dog restaurant on 120th and Federal, but then left and went to the Lazy dog off 144th and I-25. Over dinner, they discussed fitness. Chris never mentioned the Rockies Game.

They told each other they loved one another. He sent her flowers and cards and became very attached in the short time they were dating. Her friends never knew about him. She was not certain about what they talked about for 111 minutes over the phone, just a couple of hours before Shanann got home late after her flight was delayed.

She heard a television in the background of that call, she did remember, but he was not in the basement because there was no television in the basement. Also, during that call, she said he talked about him going to the field first thing Monday morning and not the office, which was not uncommon, and he wouldn't be seeing her that morning.

She did not have a key or the entry code to the home, nor did she have the access code to the security system. She barely talked to Chris on Sunday the 12, and she did not see him that day. She went to the museum with her family.

She remembers talking to Chris on Monday. She left work at 3 pm according to her timecard. She came home where she met her friend Jim, a platonic friend who had a key to her home. She refused to provide Jim's last name, and he knew nothing about this and did not know Chris.

Chris texted her around 3:45 and said my family was gone, and he asked her to call him. She calls him around 4 pm. The call is brief, and he tells her the police are there and that Shanann's friend Nicki called them. She assumed Shanann just took off with the kids after an argument. She knew that Shanann's purse and phone were left at the house, which she thought was "strange," but assumed she just left in a hurry.

She thought the house would be put up for sale that week. Chris wanted to go to work on Tuesday, but she told him to stay home and help the police. She recommended having a friend there if there was an argument and, if no one was available, to covertly record the encounter to protect himself. When asked about the argument Chris reported to have had with Shanann, she said she didn't know what time it started and that he woke Shanann at her request. She said Chris told her she got home around 2 am.

She said she asked Chris if he believed Shanann was pregnant, and he replied that she was showing in North Carolina, and she believed his story because Shanann may have lied about being pregnant out of spite. At this time, she thought that Shanann had left with the children. She persists, and he admits to Nichol that Shanann is pregnant, and the baby is his.

Chris shows concern for his wife and kids in these text messages. She first learned of Shanann's pregnancy on Tuesday during her lunch break, when she reviewed the media. She recalls primarily texting Chris on Tuesday and does not recall speaking to him on the phone.

Chris asked if Shanann's pregnancy ruined everything in their relationship. She told him that she knew that the baby belonged to him and that the baby was not from an affair Shanann was having. She confronted him and told him to stop lying. She assured him that they were okay and that he needed to focus on the family. She said he did not seem to be as concerned as she thought he should be. This was when she started to become suspicious.

She asked Chris to delete his text message from Nichol to keep their relationship a secret from his friends. She asked him what he had done, and he said he had done nothing. She told him that if he had done something that it would run both of their lives. Chris responded that he had not hurt his family. She said this was their last text message on Tuesday.

This was when she started to think that Chris had hurt his family because he lied to her and Shanann had not come home. She left her phone, purse, EpiPen, and car. She said she was scared because she did not know who Chris was anymore.

She recalled another conversation on Monday the 13th in which she said he had found Shanann's wedding ring. Chris asked Nichol how much she thought it was worth. She told him to pawn it, and he said he would have it appraised. It was a "nice rock."

Nichol said she saw the interview that Chris Watts gave on the porch. She said his eyes looked different like he had no soul, like he was a different man. She said she spoke to her father about it, and they decided to come to the police. She said she wished she had come in earlier but needed a few days to process what was going on.

Nichol said she was very financially stable, and Chris did not know that women like her existed. She feels that money was the biggest catalyst for this event.

She thought that if she was not in his life, his family might still be alive, but not permanently. She does not believe he just snapped. She does not believe that she was the only catalyst for the deaths of his family. She said that Chris and Shanann did not get along well, and the financial situation was also troubling.

When Koback asked her if there were any reasons why Chris would have hurt his children. The only thing that she could think of was if they had seen him killing Shanann. Chris loved his children.

A text message had been found between Charlotte and Nichol that appeared to reference that Nichol was dating another person. Charlotte is engaged to her closest friend. She was not dating anyone else, and Chris had no reason to believe that she was. She had been on eHarmony but never dated anyone.

Notes from Agent Tim Martinez from Nichol's answers to his questions:

Chris was always more into her than she was into him.

She met Chris in May or early June. Chris worked at Anadarko for 5-6 years and supervises people. Chris never complained of any medical issues. She never suspected that he had any mental or psychological issues. They were intimate very early on and remained very sexually active throughout. Chris had sent her pictures of his male anatomy and workout photos.

The last time they were intimate was at her home on the evening of August 11, before and after their dinner at the Lazy Dog Restaurant.

The only stressors in their marriage that she saw were that Shanann did not let him openly communicate and the financial issue.

Shanann would talk down to Chris in front of the children, which bothered him, especially when the girls started to mimic this behavior. If Chris asked Shanann for anything, she would tell him to shut up, and he didn't know anything. When the children would repeat this, it made him very sad, and he knew he had to separate from her.

Chris always told her that Shanann was a good mom. There was never any evidence of any abuse or concern.

Nichol asked multiple questions about the legal process and her employment with Anadarko.

No further questions were asked.

There are three more interviews and a letter between Nichols and Law enforcement. I plan to go into those in detail in written form in the future. Law enforcement spent time asking her questions based on information they received from her phone data that could be retrieved. Nichol Kessinger has not been heard of publicly other than one interview she gave to the Denver Post.

Three years after the horrific murders of Shanann, her daughters, Bella and CeCe, and her unborn son, Nico, she is still the focus of intense scrutiny on social media, especially after the Netflix documentary, American Murder: The Family Next Door. Before the premier, Nichol petitioned the court for a name change. It is not clear if the petition was granted as the file was sealed.

Chapter 13

Sermon on the Porch

As the search and rescue team goes through the house, Chris Watts speaks to reporters from the local news out front, pleading for his family's safe return. He explains that he has no idea where Shanann would take the children.

Journalist Tom Koppough interviews Chris on the front porch amidst the sound of dogs barking in the distance. He asks his name.

"Chris Watts, W-A-T-T-S."

"What's going on right now around your house?"

"Right now, it's - you got K9 units, the sheriff's department - everybody's, like, they're doing their best right now to figure out, like, if they can get a scent and see where they went. They went on foot, and they went in a car, they went somewhere. Right now, it's just, like, they've been on point. They're going through the house trying to get a scent, and hopefully, they

can pick something up where it's going to lead to something."
He describes, "What happened when your wife came home?

Talk to me." Koppough demands.

"She came home from the airport, 2 a.m. I left around 5:15.
She was still here.

About 12:10 that afternoon, her friend Nicole showed up
at the door. Like I had texted Shanann a few times that day, I
called her. But she never got back to me. But she wasn't getting
back to any of her people as well, and that's what really concerned a lot of people. If she doesn't get back to me, that's fine,
like she gets busy during the day. But she didn't get back to
her people, which was very concerning. Nicole called me when
she was at the door, and that's when I came home, and then
walked in the house and nothing, it's vanished. *Nothing* was
here- I mean, she wasn't here; the kids weren't here. Nobody
was here." He struggles with his pronouns.

"What's your wife's name?" "Shanann. S-H-A-N-A-N-N."

"What's your kid's name?"

"Bella and Celeste." He swallows hard." How old are your
daughters?"

"Bella's four, and Celeste is three." His blink rate accelerates
as he moistens his lips.

"So, how many times did you try calling her?" Koppough
asks.

"So, I called her three times, texted her about three times just to say what's going on." He raises his eyebrows as if looking for approval that this is an adequate number. He explains that she just got back from a trip to Arizona, and he figured she was just busy. The camera is zoomed in close enough to reveal a half-moon-shaped red mark on the left side of his neck.

"When her friend showed up - it registered. Like, this isn't right.' Chris explains.

"Do you think she just took off?" asks Koppough.

"Right now, I don't just want to throw anything, like, out there. I hope that she's somewhere safe right now and with the kids. Could she have just taken off? I don't know. But if somebody has her, and they're not safe. I want them back, now! That's what's in my head. If they're safe right now, they're going come back. But if they're not safe right now, that's the not knowing part. Last night, I had every light in the house on. I was hoping I would get, just, ran over by the kids running in the door and just barrel rushing me. But it didn't happen. It was just a traumatic night trying to be here." He swallows.

"I am going to ask you some tough questions," Koppough warns, as Chris nods and sucks in his lips as if subconsciously trying not to reveal too much about what he knows. "Your relationship with your kids...."

"My kids are my life. I mean, those smiles light up my life. He continues, describing dinner time without them and how traumatic it was for him that they weren't there, as if he was a victim. "It was tearing me apart last night." He chuckles nervously.

He describes going into their rooms and the bedtime routine he would not be performing. He smiles and says he just wants everyone to come home. He explains that she came home late from her business trip because her flight was delayed due to storms. His arms are crossed tightly across his chest, and he begins rocking from side to side in a self-soothing motion. He talks about how he left for work early that morning, and she had barely gotten in bed.

"This might be a tough question. Did you guys get into an argument before..."

"It wasn't like an argument. We had an emotional conversation." He offers. "I'll leave it at that. I just want them back." He is smiling, again, at this point of the interview. "If they're not safe right now, that's what's tearing me apart. If they are safe, then they're coming back. But if they're not, this-this-this has got to stop. Like somebody has to come forward." He pleads as if he is speaking to whoever has taken his wife and daughters.

The reporter asks about her family and what law enforcement is saying. Chris says he is hopeful now that the K9 units are searching.

"If your wife can see this if she can watch this, what would you like to tell your wife?"

He looks at the camera. "Shanann, Bella, Celeste." He blinks hard as he says his daughter Bella's name. "If you're out there, just come back. Like, if somebody has her, just please bring *her* back. I need to see everybody." His eyes are closed at that last statement. "I need to see everybody. This house is not complete without anybody here. *Please, bring them back.*" His eyes are pleading as he looks squarely at the camera. He looks westward down the street as if he sees them leaving in that direction.

Another news outlet has the chance to ask him some questions in front of the garage, away from the barking K9 units searching his home.

"I'll just wait for you to ask questions, but, like, it's...I want-I want them, wherever they are, like, at, like, I have no inclination to where they're at right now. Like, I've exhausted like every friend that I know of, and every friend that I have has called friends that Shanann has that maybe I didn't know about. And it's just like there's just like...vanished like she's not, like, when I got home yesterday, I was like a ghost town. Like, she wasn'there, kids weren't here. Like I have no idea where they went." He stammers.

He continues, "And it doesn't, just earth-shattering. I feel like this isn't even real right now. It's like a nightmare that I just can't wake up from." Chris' face is completely relaxed; his voice is monotone. He licks his lips.

"Chris, when did you learn that they weren't here?" the reporter asks.

"Yes, well, I texted her a few times, called her. I didn't get a response. Which that was a little off. Then, her friend Nickole showed up a little after noon. I saw her on the doorbell camera. I was like, 'Hey, what's going on?' She's like, 'Hey, I can't get a hold of Shanann,' and that's when I was just, like, something's not right." He looks off to the left. "She's not answering the door, and she said the car was here. It's like, I got to go home, and we got here, got inside, and nobody was here. Not- nothing." He shrugs and looks off to the right. His voice is still calm and relaxed. He licks his lips again.

"So, I read that Shanann hadn't taken the girls to school, which was unusual?"

"Yeah, because, like Bella was going to start kindergarten next-next Monday, and they were just getting ready to start-start back again." He sucks in his lips.

"So, your friend, Nickole, kind of tipped you off, that something is...."

Chris nods, "Yeah, it's like she was here at the front door and that's when I kind of knew, okay, if she's not answering anybody else either...this is- this isn't like her because, I mean, she works that direct sales business and that's her. That's what she does. And for her not to respond to any of her people. That, I mean if she doesn't respond to me, I'm like she's busy. She's got stuff going on. But, not to respond to her people, though, that was, that was not like her." He moistens his lip again.

"Chris, you've got a beautiful family." Chris blinks slowly, keeping his eyes closed for an extra moment as he asks about his loved ones. "It looks like you all love each other very much. What went through your mind the minute you are kind of like, 'something's wrong?'" the reporter asks.

Chris swallows hard and takes a short, deep breath in. "Like, I was trying to get home as fast as I can." His voice sounds helpless at this statement. "I was blowing through stoplights, and I was blowing through everything, just trying to get home as fast as I can because none of this made sense." The slight smile on his face seems out of place considering the situation.

"Like, if she wasn't here, where did she go? Once I got here, it was like, alright, who can I call? Who do I know that she could be with right now? If she went to a friend's house, where could she be staying? And we went through everybody. Just like everything in my contact list and her friend's contact list and nothing has come up. Everybody has said, like, they haven't heard from her either. I'm just hoping, right now, that she's somewhere safe." He shakes his head, "And maybe she's just- she's there. But right now, it's just like if she's vanished, like, I want her back, so, I want *those kids* back." His voice breaks; he smiles widely, licks his lips, swallows, and hugs his arms tightly against his chest.

"I want to ask you a little bit about the hard part. Your first thought is, 'Where are they? I want them back,' your second thought is, your afraid people think you may have done something?" The reporter pulls no punches.

Chris' voice again sounds helpless, "Yeah, I mean, nothing-nothing. Everybody's going to have an opinion on anything like this. I just want them people to know that I want my family back. Like, I want them safe. I want them here." He looks directly into the camera. "This house is not the same. Last night was traumatic, last night was... I-I can't really stay in this house again with nobody here. Last night, I wanted that knock on the door. I wanted to see those kids running, running, just-just barrel rush me. Just give me a hug and knock me on the ground." He is shaking his head. "But that didn't happen." He licks his lips again.

"Who are you going to stay with tonight?"

"Probably my friends Nick and Amanda. I mean, unless something develops in the next- next hours or so. Like, I'm hoping somebody sees something or somebody knows something and comes forward."

"What's the hardest part of all this for you?"

"Not knowing." He barely lets the reporter finish the question. "Like if they're safe, or...." He looks off to the left. "Or if they're in trouble. There's that- it's that variable. Like, I'm not sure. I mean, I can't do anything right now from where I'm at."

He goes on to explain that he has a doorbell camera, and the neighbor has security cameras. He is asked if all the doors were locked, to which he replies that the front and back doors were locked; however, the garage door was unlocked, which is not uncommon.

"So, how would she have left the house?" the reporter tries to understand.

"I don't want to put anything out there. Like, s-suspecting...somebody pulled in the back. We have a driveway back there from the new townhomes, but it's so hard to tell. Like there's no cameras in the backyard - It's hard to suspect if someone came and picked her up or somebody took her." you've got cops there, cops here, cops in your house, K9 units...."

"I've never seen something like this in my lifetime unless it was on TV or a movie. This doesn't seem real at all. It just seems like I'm living in a nightmare, and I can't get out of it. I just want them home so bad."

He is asked if he saw his wife when she got home from Arizona.

"I saw her when she got in, but it was really quick. It was 2 a.m. I saw the kids in the monitor before I left, and that was it." He says, with another long blink. He commends the Frederick police department for its efforts in the search for his family.

He divulges that the dogs got a scent. "Hopefully, they can pick up something and kind of go in a direction...." He looks westward, down the street.

"Describe your girls to us."

He refolds his arms across his chest, "Celeste, she's just a ball of energy, she's called rampage...she's got two speeds: go, or she's sleeping. She's always the troublemaker. She's always the one, like jumping off things, you know. Bella, she's the more calm, cautious, mothering type. She's more like me." He laughs.

"She's calmer, but Celeste- she's definitely got her mom's personality where she's always just gung-ho, ready to go!"

"You guys have a baby on the way."

"Mhmm." Chris clenches his jaw, and his smile quickly fades.

"Is that kind of going through your mind, too?"

"It's like, that's why I need *everybody* back here and *everybody* safe."

Chapter 14

Digital Footprint

Meanwhile, as the search and rescue teams were arriving at 2825 Saratoga Trail to investigate the disappearance of Shanann, Bella, and Celeste Watts, CBI Intelligence Analyst Jillian Ganley contacts Baumhover to help with the Missing Endangered Alert. Baumhover also requested assistance from CBI Agents Tammy Lee, Kevin Koback, Greg Zentner, Matthew Sailor, and Stacy Galbraith under Agent in Charge Kirby Lewis. Shortly after arriving at Frederick Police Department, they are joined by FBI Special Agents Grahm Coder and Kevin Hoyland. They receive the briefing from Baumhover and Commander David Egan.

Baumhover goes over the synopsis of the events that had occurred starting at 1:36 pm the previous day when they received a call from Nickole Atkinson requesting the welfare check of her friend Shanann Watts and her two daughters. He outlined how Nickole and her son arrived, and no one answered the door, despite Shanann's car being in the garage. Nickole knew the code to the front door, but it was latched from the inside, which heightened her concern. She did not know the garage door pin pad code, and when Shanann's husband, Christopher, finally arrived, and opened the garage door with the opener inside his work truck.

Baumhover also details that the next-door neighbor had motion-activated surveillance of Christopher backing his truck up into the garage approximately one foot. Hence, the tailgate area was not visible. Both the next-door neighbor and the Reporting Party found it to be out of the ordinary. He also advises that Chris had given consent to three searches of the house in which they discovered Shanann's wedding ring, wallet, phone, and medications were all found inside the residence. He also advises there is a GPS on Chris' work truck, and he was awaiting the records from Anadarko Petroleum Corporation.

After the briefing, the agents discuss the plan going forward that day. CBI Tammy Lee would investigate the GPS data, along with FBI Special Agents Coder and Boylan. She also contacts Nickole Atkinson to request a formal interview. Nickole, under pressure from work and family obligations, on top of the disappearance of her good friend, seems reluctant at first but is willing to meet with investigators at her place of employment.

CBI Agent Matthew Sailor would be interviewing the Lindstrom's, the neighbors who hosted a birthday party on Sunday, August 12, the day before the family disappeared. Agent Koback would interview Lindstrom's teenage daughter, who babysat for the children on Saturday, August 11. Agent Zentner would interview Nickole Atkinson at work. Special Agent Coder would conduct the formal interview with Chris Watts.

Intelligence Agent Ganley would be working on the phone records and social media accounts.

Everything we do these days is chronicled on social media. This is especially true in this case. Shanann used social media to promote her business and, in essence, the American dream. She was a charismatic, hard-working, beautiful, and well-loved member of the community. She had so many friends and family who loved her dearly, and they were all communicating on social media, trying to figure out what happened to this woman and her adorable daughters. It has become clear that Shanann did not leave of her own volition. Despite his best efforts in complying with the investigation, it has become clear that Chris Watts was somehow involved, not only to law enforcement but also to everyone in Shanann's circle of family and friends. Now that Chris Watts has given media interviews, the world will soon know as well.

Chris' truck's GPS shows us exactly where he drove and how long he was at each location. Law enforcement will soon have those records and the phone records, including the health data from Shanann and Chris' cell phones. Law enforcement can see how many footsteps they took and flights of stairs they climbed for each of them, too. For example, we know that Shanann took three stairs between midnight and 1:51 am that morning. We can also see that; conversely, Chris climbed no flights of stairs that morning.

All this digital information has given the investigators of this case a tremendous portrait of the events that transpired that day. They have the evidence. They have that portrait in their possession, and it's up to them to decide how long they study it and which parts they choose to focus on it.

Chapter 15

The Red Car

Arguably, the most crucial piece of metadata in the investigation of the disappearance of Shanann and her two young daughters, Bella, and Celeste, is the security footage from the next-door neighbor, Nate. We see Chris Watts venturing back and forth into his garage that morning. He said he was loading up tools so often that it raised suspicion for his next-door neighbor.

Weld County District Attorney, Michael Rourke, said he was loading up the deceased bodies of his family into the truck one by one. Thanks to countless emails sent to Mr. Rourke after seeing my videos on the shadow under the truck, we now know this is not the case. Thankfully, Mr. Rourke admitted that his statement to the court on November 19, the day Chris Watts was sentenced to spend the rest of his life in prison, without the possibility of parole, was made in error.

He believes at least one of the children was alive that morning. I agree; at *least* one member of his family was still alive that morning as he prepared to drive to Cervi 3-19.

I became somewhat of an expert at inspecting CCTV camera footage as a pub owner in England. I would monitor my security camera meticulously, looking for people possibly carrying knives and other weapons into my establishment. I became quite skilled at it and considered it my main talent for investigating true crime.

I used this talent to view Nate's security footage, over and over, dozens, if not hundreds of times. I showed the world the shadow under the truck, which changed the case and vindicated Shanann from the unimaginable accusations from her husband that she had murdered the children.

That is only the beginning of what I have discovered in the nearly three years since this case first made international headlines. You have not read about my discoveries in the mainstream media. I am just a man in England. I am not a professional investigator. I am not law enforcement or even a private investigator, but I see things that most everyone else has missed.

My discoveries have been viewed over 25 million times on YouTube when I am writing this book, and millions of times, people have been shown things to which the news media and law enforcement have turned their heads. Viewers of my channels have continued alerting the Weld County officials of these massive new clues. However, in my opinion, they refuse to acknowledge these findings, in part, to avoid the future embarrassment of their mishandling of this case.

At 5:18 am on Monday, August 13, 2018, Nate's motion-activated security camera is set off when Chris Watts walks out to his truck. In fact, the first minute alone of this film reveals things that law enforcement should scrutinize, as we have done on the Armchair Detective. We see someone, presumed to be Chris Watts, walk out of the garage. Seconds before his truck backs in, we see a car pull out from beyond the Watts driveway.

Some would say this is just the neighbor to the west, pulling out to go to the gym, as she did each morning. However, the neighbor to the west drives a gray car, and the car we see in the film is red. Bette has kindly conveyed to me that she turned left, heading west down Saratoga Trail that morning.

This red car accelerates straight ahead at rapid speed, heading north down Steeple Rock Drive. It is actually quite impressive the planning and execution of this sequence of events. We do see Bette's grey car pull out and turn left, and with military precision, we see the red car pull out at nearly the same moment, without braking, headed straight ahead.

As impressive as the synchronicity of these events may be, as near to the same moment as these cars pulled out, it was not the same moment. The film is there in the public domain to review and scrutinize, and we have done. Law enforcement has seen this footage and was fooled. I was not fooled.

The driver of the red car was waiting for Bette to pull out in hopes of avoiding detection. For his part, Chris Watts knew about Nate's camera, at least the one pointed toward his driveway. Likewise, he knew Bette's morning routine; she left every day between 5:00 and 5:15 am to go to the gym.

Later that afternoon, as Nate shows officer Coonrod and Chris the footage, we see Chris Watts begin to panic. At that moment, a red car pulls out we s. Wehim become flustered, unconsciously look toward the exit, and place his hands on top of his head to try to get more oxygen to his body, much like a runner at the end of a race. He makes several large gestures with his hands and arms, trying to divert the attention away from the screen, and checks his phone.

Who is the driver of the red car? Why did Chris have this reaction the moment he saw the red car pull out?

Chapter 16

Female Silhouette

The neighbors' security films have given us answers to many questions. It is important to note that there is a delay from when the motion is detected to when the recording begins. I have seen home security customers speak of significant delays due to the camera resetting between recordings in my research.

This may explain why Officer Coonrod saw Nickole pulling away from the Watts' home after dropping off Shanann after her business trip but not seeing her pulling in on Nate's recordings. That being stated, we must consider the possibility that the footage beginning at 5:18 on Monday, August 13, when we see the figure walking out of the garage just before the red car drives off and before the truck is backed in, maybe on a delay due to the settings chosen by the owner of the security system as well as the delays when the camera resets between motions detected.

It is also important to mention that the Weld County discovery states that the truck backs in at 5:27 am, which directly conflicts with the bodycam footage of Nate's T.V., which clearly shows the truck backed up at 5:18 a.m.

I have analyzed this footage more times than any other CCTV footage in my life, and I am going to walk you through exactly what I have seen. The figure walking out of the garage is dressed in a black long-sleeve shirt with the sleeves pulled down and straight-leg jeans. This is consistent with the clothes seen by Christopher Watts later in the video in the daylight.

That is where the similarities end, in my opinion. Watts wears his sleeves pushed up, bearing his forearms. Watts has on black boots. Watts has very short hair and a beard. Watts is a man.

Gait analysis is the systematic study of limb movement. In China, there is a new surveillance tool called gait recognition. This technology identifies individuals by their body shapes and how they walk, even when their faces are hidden.

This cutting-edge technology is used to help fill the gaps in facial recognition software where the face is not visible.

The length of the stride differs by a margin of at least half of a foot. The most important feature that differentiates these two individuals is the foot strike on the ground. The female individual's foot strike is mid-foot dominant, having what is referred to as an early flat stance, whereas Watts has a pronounced heel roll. In simple terms, the female walks without striking her heel, which is common for people who wear heels and wedges.

Chris Watts has a very pronounced heel strike, both in boots and in the prison, issue shoes, which have a considerably softer heel, much like a moccasin, as he describes. These rule out the argument that Watts walks differently because he is not wearing boots in the 5:18 footage.

They say a picture is worth a thousand words. If you were to look at a still frame of the female individual from 5:18 am and zoom in, as I have done, you would notice several very note-worthy things. I assert that the female individual has a higher collar on her top, wears her hair in a high ponytail with her long, dark hair cascading down her back, is shorter in stature than Watts, lacks the full dark beard of Watts, and has a more rounded posterior.

Furthermore, we can see the shadow cast by this individual on the driveway. If you were to look at this person's shadow and rotate it upright, you would see a shapely female silhou-ette. Chris Watts had been focused on his fitness transfor-mation in the months prior. He changed his eating habits to a macronutrient-based diet, increased his exercise, and sub-scribed to the Thrive lifestyle marketed by Shanann. He lost a reported 70 pounds, or 31.75 kilograms, transforming his physique into a lean V-shape with broad chest and shoulders tapering down to a narrow waist and hips.

The 5:18 am figure's shadow not V-shaped, but a more hour-glass shape that tapers in at the waist then out at the hips. Shanann had shoulder-length hair, was pregnant, and presumed to be deceased at this time, ruling her out as the woman walking out the garage that morning, which begs the question: who is this mystery woman?

Chapter 17

The Shadow Man

It was January 10, 2019, when I aired my series *Watts in the Shadows.* When asked, I named this first video as my favorite, because, in my opinion, it changed the case. Serendipitously, this aired on what would have been Shannan's 37th birthday, which I did not know at the time. I will never forget this date.

I presented these findings in three videos. The first one was the overall effect; Chris Watts was on the right of the screen and the shadow walked to him from the left. He bent down to pick it up and put it in the cab.

I seemed to convince most viewers that this was the shadow of a second human being, but I did not convince everyone. So, in the second video, I tried to convince some of the doubters. Chris is near the driver's side of the truck and a smaller second shadow walks from the garage and over to Watts. Did this shadow belong to one of the girls? If my findings were correct, this debunks Chris' confession to special agent Grahm Coder of the FBI and CBI investigator Tammy Lee as utter nonsense. More importantly, it vindicates Shanann Watts of any culpability in the deaths of her daughters.

126

These videos were aired two and a half years ago at the time I am writing this book. The quality of the videos is not as clear as those I have aired more recently. My investigative team has more sophisticated equipment now, and we have been able to digitally enhance the sound and the picture quality of these CCTV videos. Even then, the images were clear enough to convince thousands of viewers. The result was an influx of emails to the district attorney's office.

On February 18 of 2019, Coder, Lee, and Baumhover travel to Wisconsin to pay Watts a visit in prison. According to Lee, the purpose of the visit was to interview Christopher Watts regarding the deaths of his wife and children, as well as to discuss other individuals claiming to have had relationships with Chris during his marriage to Shanann.

Lee reports that the reason was to interview Watts about Trent and Amanda, two people who claimed to have had sexual relationships with Watts while he was married. I believe this was a cover and the real reason the three made the trip was to get the real confession from Chris, considering the new information sent to the district attorney regarding the shadow under the truck.

In a newspaper article published on March 7, 2019, the reporter remarks that investigators believe this confession to be *most* credible. D.A. Rourke indicates that the CCTV footage evidence of the small shadow under the truck matches this new confession.

Rourke says that this new evidence is consistent with his new account of his two young daughters being alive that morning.

It must not have been easy for Rourke to admit that he was wrong and that he did not actually see Chris loading the bodies of his family into his truck that morning. His statement during the sentencing was false. He lied to the public, and more importantly, he lied to the families.

I believe that the Armchair Detective changed the case and helped to clear Shanann's name. Surprisingly, there are content creators that still, to this day, assert that Shanann Watts murdered her children. After all these revelations, they still cling to Watt's original confession from August 15. 2018. I find this to be deeply disturbing. What's even more disturbing is that people subscribe to these channels and their theories without considering the impact the shadow videos have on this case.

Furthermore, there are other channels that claim to have seen the shadow before I did. I released my findings to the public on January 10, 2019. Just over a month later, the investigators were re-interviewing Watts in Wisconsin, and a few weeks later, D.A. Rourke admitted the girls were alive that morning. That is the sequence of events. That is the truth. That is why they call me, Alan Vinnicombe, the Shadow Man.

What is most intriguing is that while making my video on the shadow I used the words "bends down and picks up the shadow and puts it in the truck."Mr. Rourke used almost the same words during his interview after the second visit with Watts.

I will not carry on about it; I am not too concerned with receiving the credit for finding the shadow under the truck, because I know it is the truth and anyone who reads this book can look up the facts that I have outlined here and verify for themselves. Admittedly, I am affected by the haters who call me a liar and a scammer, those who post negative or threatening comments on YouTube.

I try not to let it affect me and my moderators, or spanners, as I refer to them, are very good at deleting disrespectful comments in the chat, in the comments section on YouTube, and on Facebook. The Armchair Detective team has zero-tolerance for rudeness or threats.

Chapter 18

More Questions than Answers

1. Nates CCTV has a 10-second delay. Chris activated it coming out and then it recorded the 2nd person coming out of the garage.

2. The doorbell cam did show Shanann's phone screen as she walked in. Her phone did pick up on the home router and it appears the kids were not in their bed.

3. The house was immaculate everywhere except her office.

4. The red car went straight. The red appearance is not from Chris's taillights. If it were, how did it make the complete rear of the car red?

5. How does one explain the alerts in the house such as the TV turning on after Chris left and the alert about the interior garage door?

6. Cervi - the grave was not disturbed on Wednesday night even after a torrential rainstorm on Tuesday night.

7. Clothes in the blue bag - equals the possibility of being the accomplices' clothes. Were these clothes meant to be worn during the ride to Cervi in the Lexus?

8. The mistresses' phone pinged the morning of the murders from the Frederick cell tower.

9. The entire plan was ruined because Shanann changed her password on her phone.

10. Why would Chris take his family to the oil site?

11. No Lexus, no plan, last place you would hide bodies.

12. Didn't act alone, 4 people.

13. 4 people- CW truck, gray truck, Lexus, truck out the back, and the red car.

14. Had to rearrange the plan and throw Chris under the bus.

15. Rourke said Chris hid the bodies to never be found but was found so quickly - equals my belief that that was not the original place to put them.

16. The first shadow released was not found by me and was of a woman carrying a child. This must have been photoshopped.

17. AD and his team's opinion are that Chris did not act alone.

18. There are many things left to make you aware of that indeed point to others being there.

19. I will continue to show every detail of this case in the next few books in this series.

20. One major suspected motive was the 2 prior explosions at Meade and Firestone.

21. Was this entire thing a setup for money from another explosion?

22. A missing person case can collect insurance money for 10 years.

23. Why did he take the blame?

24. Who is he hiding?

25. Will the truth ever come out?

26. One day we hope to talk with Chris about the truth.

27. The cover-up...

28. Why was the crime scene shut down within 2 hours?

29. Why didn't LE confirm the confession?

30. Why did they believe a confirmed liar?

31. Is it because it suited LE? - why? coverup?

Chapter 19

The Clock Stopped

Agent Tammy appeared on Oxygen in an episode called Criminal Confessions. It aired in December 2019. She stated that this was one of the worst cases she had seen in 19 years.

Tammy was shocked to hear Chris confess to his dad. "It was the theme I had just given him before leaving the room," Tammy tells Oxygen.

They knew that getting Chris's dad into the interview room was extremely risky for Tammy and Grahm. Tammy said they didn't know where Ronnie's head was. The fear set in that Ronnie could come in and convince Chris to get a lawyer.

"It was a split-second decision if we were going to let Ronnie into the room," Tammy says she and Grahm went to talk with Ronnie first and instructed him on what to do.

"Time was of the essence for us to get back in there so we could redirect the interview and try and get more of the facts."
Tammy had a lot of work already planned for this case. She had several interviews that still needed to be conducted. All

the evidence had not been looked at when Chris stopped the clock when he pleaded guilty.

The local district attorney's office had full control at this point. Frederick Police had invited the CBI and FBI in to help this case. The DA's office was the entity that was controlling these outside investigators.

On Wednesday, August 15th, 2018, at 10:12 pm, Officer Walje, Officer Manley, Sgt. Bakes and Officer Lines entered the "crime scene" at the home on Saratoga Trail. At 11:12 pm, the Weld County Chief Deputy District Attorney, Steve Wrenn, and Deputy district attorney, Patrick Roche, arrived.

On page 129 of the discovery, it is noted that the front door was closed and locked at 12:11 am. The time spent on the triple homicide that allegedly occurred at 2825 Saratoga Trail, Frederick, Colorado, lasted a total of 1 hour and 59 minutes.

The crime scene was searched, evidence collected, and released before the bodies of the deceased were recovered. My question to you is this: How is this possible?

Chris was in court on Thursday, August 16, 2018, for his first hearing. One of the first things that the defense needed the Judge to look at was a motion that information had been leaked to the press by an inside law enforcement officer.

Chris was moved to jail and placed in isolation for safety reasons. He spoke to no one.

In November of 2018, Chris Watts pled guilty to killing his wife. At this very moment, the clock stopped on every level. Tammy and Grahm were devastated. The case would be closed and await sentencing. Blindsided with the fact that the investigation had been stopped, the FBI and CBI were left holding a mountain of things that were not completed.

Vital evidence was then put into boxes and drawers and, to my knowledge, never looked at again. I don't think the DNA evidence was even sent to be processed. They collected it, but was it processed?

The DA went onward to win his reelection the day after Chris was sentenced. I believe that a certain company and person pulled off the FBI and CBI to stop certain people from having to take the stand. The evidence in the current discovery "somewhat" supports this idea.

The fact is, had this case proceeded with a full discovery period, it would have lasted up to 2 years to finish this portion. We would have learned critical inconsistencies between the major players.

Chapter 20

Closing Argument: Folie a Deux

This section of the book is based on theory.

My name is Alan, and I am the Armchair Detective.

Do you know that game where you must guess the number of marbles in a jar? Where each person guesses and submits their answers to win a prize? If you looked at the data from those submissions statistically, you would see the range will vary wildly.

For example, if the number of marbles in the jar is 585. Some people will have guesses ranging anywhere from, let's say, 208 and going as high as, say 843. So, the range would be 635. That's the difference between what one person's guess might be from another person's guess. Neither person got anywhere close to the actual number, 585, but it shows you how vastly different the answers could be.

It's familiar to this case. You have wildly different theories floating around, ranging from Shanann being drunk and murdered the children to Chris Watts being innocent. He didn't kill anyone; he was given some drug and was mind-controlled or hypnotized. Wildly different theories from the same discovery, just like the wildly different guesses for the number of marbles in the jar.

That's what happens when people's critical thinking skills are clouded by emotion or ego, or self-preservation; they tend to look at only the evidence that fits their theory and ignore the rest, just to fit what they choose to believe.

The investigators, in this case, were brilliant. They figured out very early on what had happened here. It was plainly obvious that Chris Watts was guilty to everyone. They were organized, efficient, and had the help of brilliant forensic analysts to go through the metadata from the bodycam footage, phone data, health data, choose what was relevant, put it in chronological order, and present their findings to investigators.

Tammy Lee and Grahm Coder did an amazing job cracking Chris wide open and getting him to confess to murdering Shanann. They used the Reid Technique so brilliantly to get him to confess to murdering Shanann. This was a very risky maneuver, but it worked. They got their man.

Sending Ronnie Watts into the interrogation room was also a very risky maneuver. They made a split-second decision at the risk of having Chris request his right to counsel and shutting the whole thing down. They looked at their options but were effective at analyzing the metadata and figuring out exactly what happened. They had enough evidence to get Chris to confess but more than enough to convict. They also had all the data they needed to prove that he did not act alone.

This case is closed. They shut down the investigation as soon as possible for political reasons to pacify big interest in Weld County. They had one of their suspects locked down, and that's all they needed to appease some people, including the family Shanann Watts. So that's it. Case closed?

Then why are people still talking about it, day in and day out, almost three years later? I'll tell you why. The way they shut this case down has left people with more questions than answers. This case may be "closed," but it has not been solved. That is, until now. You have people all over the world very passionate about this case and finding the answers they seek.

Do you remember that jar from the beginning of this chapter? Do you know how statistically rare it is for one person to guess the correct number of marbles? I can tell you they are very low. Did you know that when you take all the submissions together, add them up, and then divide that number by the number of guesses, the number you are left with will be much closer to the actual number of marbles in the jar?

We here at the Armchair Detective team have solved this case. Not by clinging on to conspiracy theories or going down a rabbit hole and never finding our way back out, but by sticking to discussing the case. That's what sets us apart from all the other people discussing the case on YouTube. We have looked at all the evidence objectively, filtered through it, discussed and debunked certain theories, and put together the sequence of events to point out the key facts that all lead up to the truth. Chris Watts did not act alone.

Do you remember that show Columbo with Peter Faulk? He is one of my heroes, as you probably know if you are one of my subscribers who analyze the data and take notes, discuss the case in chat, and have come to the same conclusion as me.

We have done it; we know what happened. We have laid out all the evidence in meticulous detail in this book in chronological order. We have come to the same conclusion as the investigators who worked brilliantly to show you what happened.

At the end of every episode, Columbo would go through the narrative of what happened, blowing the guilty parties away with his accuracy, and at the end of every show, the bad people go to jail.

Those watching at home could rest assured that justice was served, and the bad people were punished. Unfortunately, this is not the way it is in the real world, and sometimes the bad guy gets away.

Justice can still be served in this case, though. Sure, it has taken longer than one hour to solve this case, but we have done it. It's taken me 3 years of hard work and looking at every theory, having the discussions, interviewing witnesses and experts.

I have waited a very long time for my Columbo moment, but the time has come. Now I am prepared to explain to you exactly what happened.

Folie a` Deux

Chris Watts had help. I proved to you a woman was walking out of the garage that day. I proved to you there was a car that pulled out with military precision, obscured from sight by the truck. Whether the car is red, orange, gray, or brown, it was not Bette's car. Chris Watts is not stupid, not by any means, he lied to Shanannfor weeks about his affair with Nichol Kessinger, and I believe I have proven that they knew each other for much longer than they had let on.

He fooled Shanann and Nichol Kessinger both for so long, and they believed him for so long. He had his parents fooled into thinking that Shanann was the one who killed the kids. There are lunatics out there latching on to them, causing them to suffer by this feud with Shanann's family, with everyone on social media choosing sides and fighting with one another, going "real life," and causing so much pain and drama for everyone involved, including both families.

He convinces people of his various lies everywhere to create chaos because he is bored and angry that he got caught. He fooled law enforcement with all his so-called confessions, too many to keep track of, but we are keeping track here at the Armchair Detective. He taps into people and learns what to use to play into their sympathies and causes pain and chaos for everyone because he is evil. He convinced his prison mates into believing his lies by learning and quoting the bible. He tapped into Cheryln Cadle and convinced her some unseen evil force possessed him. He has YouTube creators bickering and arguing over these wild theories by capitalizing on his innocent guy; he was framed, he is not a smart character.

Nichol Kessinger is in hiding, afraid to show her face in public for fear of being eaten alive if anyone finds out her new identity. Reopen this case and find out who he manipulated into helping him dispose of the bodies of his wife and children because we know he did not do it alone. She came to the police of her own volition, and she is not in prison; why? Maybe it's because she is completely innocent. Set the record straight, once and for all.

He has people believing there was a cover-up, that a firestick could cause an explosion and that big oil is to blame because they are greedy and don't care about the lives of innocent people, making law enforcement look like they are all in on it.

Please reopen the case, find out who the accomplices are, and set the record straight, Mr. Rourke. You are the district attorney in Weld County, and you have the power to stop the chaos and give everyone the truth.

Please reopen the case and find us the answers we all need to walk away. You alone can set the record straight and end this social media circus and let the families heal in peace, and the beautiful souls of Shanann, Bella, Celeste, and Nico Watts. You have the power, and you can end this.

Grahm Coder said there were 2 Chris Watts. Open the file and set the record straight. You listened to me once before; please, do it one more time.

The only thing necessary for the triumph of evil is for good men to do nothing.

Alan Vinnicombe, Armchair Detective

The Shadow Man is only the beginning. I have invested hundreds if not thousands of hours with my team researching this case. This book is intended for those that have not heard about the Watts case. Those who have studied the case can now see exactly what I have questioned since the beginning. I have two more books scheduled that will continue the story of events for this case. I will be diving in deep, starting with the very minute Chris Watts is handcuffed. The hours and days that follow that moment are excruciating.

Special Thanks To My Supporters

Alana Johnson

Alecia Wikander

Alice Goodknight

Alisha Hassinger

Amanda Harris

Amanda Holland

Amanda Simson

Amy Eck

Angela Bourret

Angela Wolf Tail

Angie Nolan

Anita Jarvis

Anna Khomyak

Annette Thompson

Ashley Comer

Ashley Mathews

Barb Jefrey

Barbara Shaw

Bernadette Conway

Bethany Stump

Brenda Busby

Brianne Wilson

Bubbles Marie

Buena Cordero

CaCa

Candace Queen

Candy R.

Carrie Casey Shean

Caterina Kozier

Catherine Harvey

Cathryn Cooper

Cathy Biondo

Cecilia Balakonis

Celeste Hill

Chela McGuire

Cheryl Gilbert

Chicken Lady

Christina Spencer

Christine Clark

Christine Mimi Reck

Cindy Hobbs

Clint Taylor

Constance Bahrami

Corrina Young

Cute Dimples

Danille Dennis

Darlene Mock

Dawn Eversole

Dawn Jones

Dean Araki

Dean Jillian

Debbie Bilyeu

Debbie Crum

Debbie Smith

Debbie Swanson

Debra Biggerstaf

Dee Persinger

Denise Marchese

Derek Titus

Desirae Tafolla

Desiree Childs

Diane Mannon

Diane Pidgeon

Diggler TC

Dominique Demarco

Donna Bolton

Donna Stokes

Elizabeth F.

Elizabeth Suarez

Gama & Gramps Love J J & J

Geraldine Boyd

Ginger Garner

Görel Blennow

Hanne Sommer Andersen

Honey Bear

Jackie Winder

Jacqueline Landry

Jan Cosgrove

Jana Ferguson

Janet McPhail

Janine Delany

Janne Isabella Tobiassen

Jason Sparks

JC - Jules

Jean Carter

Jean Fischer

Jeanette Owen

Jeanne Sullivan

Jeannette Johnson

Jenn Beat

Jenna Milne

Jennifer Harvey

Jennifer Link

Jennifer O'Connor

Jennifer Vitello

Jennifer Whitus

Jenny M Little Speckled Hen

Jenny Robson

Jill Detro

Jill Fries

Jo Lynn Stich

Joan Baechler

Joanne McLean

Jodi Slaughter

Joe Camfield

John DeVries

Jonesy

Jory Zoelle

Joyce Hatcher

Judy Croft

Julie Braswell

Julie Frew

Julie Gaul

Julie Goyen

Karen Ann

Karen Boroski

Karen Darling

Karen McMullin

Karen McPadden

Karen Soucek

Kathy Voyles

Keisha Duggan

Kelly McCarty

Kelly Molde

Kenneth Knittle

Kerry Hughes

Kerryn Devlyn

Kilji Jenkins

Kimberly Edgell

Kimberly Ruzicka

Kristy Gordon

Laura Simmons

Lea Dawn Willis

Lenita Byrd

Lesley Auger

Lesley Burwell

Lina Pizzolato

Linda Coberly

Linda Dudley

Linda Williams

Lisa Shannon Baldwin

Loretta Fields

Lori Collicott

Lorrene Fontes

Lucinda Gaskill

Lynne Marie Stewart

Mandy Dawson

Margaret Driver

Margie Singer

Maria Mathews

Marie Ginter

Marilyn Chrest

Marsha Bohannon

Mary Lopez

Mary O'Connor

Mary Specht

Mary York

Maryjane Persons

Melanie Ganley

Melissa Berezowsky

Melissa Canup

Melissa Johnson

Meredith Oakes

Merryk Toro

MiA

Michele Myers

Michelle Tighe

Morag Hamilton-Reddy

Ms Thing B

N. Wright

Nancy Cougle

Nancy Schroeder

Nicola Walsh

Nita Wall

Nora Cumming

Nora Halpin

Pamela Bruns

Pamela Hart

Pamela Horsley

Pamela Nicholson

Patricia Shelton

Patti Dorsey

Paula Bailer

Rachel Wojcik

Raeanne Pike

Readings by Roxby

Rebekka Wisniewski

Raeznkane

Renee Davis O'neil

RiSa

Robert Brown

Robin Adams

Robyn Williams

Robyne Gardner

Rosanna Kallay

Rose Fauci

Ruby Morales

Sally Kirby

Sam I Am MVVP

Sandra Mullen

Sara Nicole

Sarah Roy

Scuba Gal

Shannon Baldwin

Shannon Lawson

Shari Hunt-Davis

Shawna Callaway

Shawna Foreman

Sheelagh Y-oke

Shelly Swartz

Silley Nana

Simon Osborne

Siobhan Healy

Snooper Sonja Rix

Mrs. Sonya Palin

Stacey Burnaroos

Stacy Hockett

Stephanie Ricardo

Stephanie Thompson

Spicy Chick

Susan Calhoon

Susan Devenport

Susan Hughes

Susan Primavera

Tammy Duff

Tammy Hahn

Tara Preston

Terry Thayer

Tiffany Marriotti

Tina Butler

Tina Vosberg

Toni Marshall

Tracey Dawe

Tracey Fitzgerald

Tracey Mason

Tracy Hernandez

Tracy Wheeler

Ursula O'Neill

Valerie Klopp

Veronica Warren

Vicki Fox

Virginia Ladymon

9 780578 986913